Concept of Sīla in Buddhism and Jainism

About the Author

A renowned Buddhist scholar, **Ven. Medagoda Abhayatissa** did his B.A. (1998-2002), M.A. and M.Phil. in Buddhist Studies from University of Kelaniya, Sri Lanka in 2004 and 2007 respectively. He was awarded Ph.D. in Buddhist Studies from University of Delhi (India) in 2010. He also holds a PG Diploma in Buddhist Studies (1999) and Royal Pandit (1999).

He started his career as Visiting Lecturer in the Dept. of Pali and Buddhist Studies, University of Kelaniya (Sri Lanka) in 2003. Currently he is Professor of Pali in the Department of Pali and Buddhist Studies at University of Sri Jayewardenepura (Sri Lanka).

A seasoned academic and researcher, his research interests include-Pali Literature, Pali Sutra study and composition of Pali Gathas.

Recipient of various awards and recognitions, Dr. Abhayatissa has authored many books, article collections and a number of his research papers have published in reputed journals.

He has attended many national and international seminars and conferences and presented research papers. A member of various professional bodies, he has been engaged with some research projects.

Concept of Sīla in Buddhism and Jainism

A Comparative Study

Medagoda Abhayatissa

CONCEPT PUBLISHING COMPANY PVT. LTD.
NEW DELHI-110059

ISBN: 978-93-5439-000-5

First Published 2024

Published and Printed by

Concept Since 1974

Concept Publishing Company Pvt. Ltd.
A/15-16, Commercial Block, Mohan Garden,
New Delhi-110059 (INDIA)
T : +91-11-41101460
E : publishing@conceptpub.com; *W* : www.conceptpub.com

Cataloging in Publication--Courtesy: D.K. Agencies (P) Ltd. <docinfo@dkagencies.com>

Abhayatissa, Medagoda, author.
Concept of Sīla in Buddhism and Jainism : a comparative study / Medagoda Abhayatissa.
pages cm
Includes bibliographical references and index.
ISBN 9789354390005

1. Buddhist ethics. 2. Jaina ethics. 3. Buddhist philosophy. 4. Jaina philosophy. 5. Enlightenment (Buddhism) I. Title.

LCC BJ1289.A24 2024 | DDC 294.35 23

Foreword

The core philosophy of Buddhism and Jainism is based on *Sila* (right conduct) and *Nirvana* (enlightenment). The interpretation and exposition of its concept by Buddhist and Jain scholars are easily recognigable as the greatest philosophical contribution to humanity. According to them, without the shared experience of *Sila,* individuals will face moral instability due to a breakdown in standards and values, leading eventually to disintegration of society. *Sila* is thus the music of their soul and a rainbow of their sublime thoughts, their feelings and culture and finds vivid expression in the compassion of Buddha and Mahavira and in their language of humanness, tolerance and cooperation. Arnold Toynbee rightly suggests that society is not constituted of individuals but of their relationships. It is *Sila* that provides harmony and robustness to such relationships to ensure their sustainability.

Buddhist concept of *Sila* is based on *Metta* (love), *Karuna,* (compassion) *Mudita,* (sympathetic happiness) and *Upekkha* (equanimity). Life lived according to these four virtues is known as Brahma Vihara (authentic existence). It is quite similar to the concept of morality in Jainism and hermeneutics. Gadamer, Heidegger and Aristotle's interpretation of moral conduct , to a great extent, echo the spirit of *Sila*. Gadamer follows Heidegger's analysis of the person as someone who has embedded within himself the world with its prejudices, traditions and environment and inherited a community in which he is required to make ethical judgments and engage in morally justifiable acts. Clarifying his analysis, Gadamer observes that it is a reality that individual can never fully escape from and points out that Aristotelian concept of a virtuous man can be understood better only in the context of the situation in which he lives and reacts. The ethical norms of such a man are neither abstract nor ethereally discrete. Instead, he exudes positive thoughts while determining his answer to the question, 'what should I do'? Thus, the ethics of hermeneutics, Buddhists and Jains manifests in life itself, harmonizing the philosophical and practical character of human beings and their behaviour.

Sila needs to be evaluated both in the socio-historical context and by giving importance to the inner voice of our beings which help modify our thoughts and respond to social and political situations appropriately. Like the hermeneutics of Socrates which seeks to comprehend the true meaning and purpose of life, *Sila's* understanding of human beings is both ethical and pragmatic whose moral values are not conditioned by prejudices of his community but by its inherent sense of rights, justice and tolerance.

The human history has been an exercise in moral dialectics, in which morality has transformed pagans into civilized members of the society. Among the ancients, this process was majorly influenced by spiritual awakening. The Stoics believed that man must suffer and bear misfortunes of destiny with equanimity, meaning that he must develop a sense of resignation and quiet acceptance. But Buddhists and Jains thought otherwise. *Sila,* for them, was not a private occupation but an active principle that encouraged freedom, growth of scientific temper and a moral drive to take the human civilization forward. Indian Society in the 6th century BC was beset with superstitions and ignorance that continue to afflict us even today. It was Buddha and Mahavira who awakened the dormant divinity in the human beings and their spirit of public service so that a society that is both moral and dynamic is created and preserved. History has repeatedly proven that its course is not conditioned merely by political dispensations but by inherent wisdom and virtue of humans. Only those norms and values remain relevant in time which foster moral symmetry and reciprocity among human beings. Bertrand Russell's views are quite relevant in this respect. He writes, "To understand an age or a nation, we must understand its philosophy and to understand its philosophy we must ourselves be in some degree, philosophers. There is here a reciprocal causation: the circumstances of men's life do much to determine their philosophy, but conversely, their philosophy do not determine their circumstances much."

The Buddhist patriarchs and Jain Triratnas have defined life as a narrative of cosmic drama in which Dhamma forms the essence. Dhamma controls, guides and regulates the human life and calls upon individuals to undergo rigorous discipline and pass though the wheels of fire (cycle of birth and death) to experience Nirvana (Summon Bonum). All philosophies and related science have since been exploring mystery of the dialectic of birth and death. According to Plato, "dialectic is the only procedure which proceeds by the destruction of assumptions to the very first principle, so as to give itself a firm base". Philosophy, Science and Truth, he explains, are the Absolute Good and dialectic helps in perceiving the Absolute Good. It is by pursuing Absolute Good that dialectic is able to dispense with the hypotheses of the mathematicians, who assume that reality, as opposed to appearance, is completely and perfectly Good and to perceive the Good, therefore, is to perceive reality.

Throughout Plato's philosophy there is a fusion of intellect and mysticism as in Pythagoreanism, where mysticism has an edge. Significantly, his concept of Absolute Good has a striking resonance in the Buddhist and Jain concept of *Sila*. Plato attaches great importance to intuition which helps an individual experience the transcendental nature of enlightenment, known as mysticism. Kant calls the dialectical understanding of the moral value systems 'Categorical Imperative', which entails that one must 'act only according to the rule of conduct that has the potential to become universal law'. He introduces Deontological concept to explain that morality must be binding on everybody so that "you treat humanity, whether in your own person or in that of another, always as an end and never as a means only." His concept of 'Categorical Imperative' and *Sila* of Buddhists and Jains were never more relevant than in the present time.

Moral doctrines have been interpreted by different thinkers at different periods of history differently but they mostly hover around two basic postulates - descriptive and normative. The anthropologists refer morality in a descriptive sense, meaning that moral values comprise of a code of conduct which society practices. In normative sense, the moral code of conduct is accepted by all social systems due largely to intellectual and volitional compulsions. According to them, moral norms warrant that code of conduct can determine interpersonal interactions but they must be rational and not harmful to others.

In recent times, radical changes have taken place in understanding moral values, precepts and prescriptions. Scientific scrutiny is invariably applied and inquiries are made before justifying any moral systems. Thinkers of today who have grown with developments in human sciences have started questioning the very fundamentals of moral values, sanctioned by religious and social systems. The radical ones among them have rejected even some of the religious values and norms that were advocated in the west by Church during the period of Reformation and Renaissance in 16th century. If we examine the Buddhist and Jain concept of *Sila* in the background of recent scientific and technological advancements, the inherent flaws in the radicals' thought process become quite obvious.

By propounding *Sila,* Buddhism and Jainism lay down sound ethical foundation for living beings and their enlightenment. The radicals interpret *Sila* as a historical necessity but the truth is that unless humanity accepts and follows compassion and non-violence embedded in *Sila*, the end of our glorious civilization is imminent. Buddhism and Jainism also reject the doctrine of 'Providence of God' as the main driving force behind all historical events, nor do they accept history as an expression of theological dictum since it does not provide the valid and authentic truth. History, according to them, is neither an account of Marxist dialectical materialism nor of the Hegelian spirit but it is a narrative of origin and development of *Sila* (value system) in different civilizations that have enriched the cultural contents of social systems and kept them alive and vibrant. Further, the structure of society is essentially based on ethical norms and values which cannot be undermined for creating a better world.

Buddhism and Jainism also reject the dangerous Pyrrhonism (extreme skepticism). Today, the world faces impending threats from nuclear and cybernetic powers that are geared to control our communications, our life and means of sustenance. *Sila* becomes extremely relevant in this context. Unless these destructive forces are anchored around compassion (Karuna) and non – violence (Ahimsa), all forms of life are bound to become extinct from the planet earth. The present civilization has in fact become Faustian. The scientific and technological advance is no doubt irreversible but they need to be sublimated to the highest sense of morality. There is no denying that public spirit and public service are desirable instruments for social progress but they need to be nourished by *Sila* so that it remains constructive and virtuous. The very survival of human civilization is also threatened today by largescale degradation of ecological environments. This downhill can only be arrested if we accept *Sila* in all its manifestations. The ethical teachings of the Buddha and Mahavira is in essence the panacea of the present crisis, our civilization confronts and become a harbinger of the dawn of an era of renaissance, characterized by humanism.

We are witnessing a fundamental change in the worldview of society and philosophy particularly in the way we perceive morality and human existence. According to Fritjof Capra, "the paradigm consists of a number of ideas and values, among them the view of the universe as a mechanical system composed of elementary building blocks, the view of the human body as a machine, the view of life as a competitive struggle for existence, the belief in unlimited material progress to be achieved through economic and technological growth, and last but not the least – the belief that a society in which the female is everywhere subsumed under the male is one that is ' natural'. During recent decade, all these assumptions have been found to be severely flawed, calling for radical revision." That we must act morally is what Immanuel Kant also advocates forcefully. These ideas have led to objective science becoming more humane and epistemic. Werner Heisenberg, one of the founding fathers of quantum mechanics, believes that 'in the drama of existence we are both choreographer and spectator. In this process, our observation of nature invariably gets modified and tinged.' He has thus introduced subjectivism in scientific investigation. Unlike him, worldview of Buddhism is imbedded deeply in moral awareness, based on Dhamma.

A thorough evaluation of hermeneutics, metaethics and deontological doctrine should leave no doubt in our mind that the doctrine of *Sila* is even more relevant today than at the time of Buddha and Mahavira. Man is a unit of value and the civilization is a sum total of his value. Over the years, the western civilization has been charred by racial, religious and economic prejudices, violence and disharmony which leave us occasionally wondering whether moral doctrines emphasized by Buddha and Mahavira is relevant at all. But we must not forget that it is their message of peace, reconciliation, love, compassion and non- violence that hold hope for the survival of humanity. Buddha drives home the ultimate truth by espousing that 'enmity cannot be conquered by enmity but only through empathy and non- violence.' This is what he calls eternal Dhamma.

Abhayatissa's book The Concept of *Sila* in Buddhism and Jainism is a very comprehensive study and understanding of *Sila* as explained in the canonical literatures of Buddhism and Jainism. It is an outstanding research work that enables readers to have a deep insight into what constitutes ethical crisis that world confronts today and how to find ways to deal with them. This seminal work could come only from Abhayatissa who is a renaissance monk of Sri Lanka. By presenting the semantics of Buddhism in a completely new light, he has indeed emerged as a new Buddhist patriarch.

October 15, 2021 **Prof. L.P. Singh**
New Delhi

Preface

The present work is substantially based on the findings of my research on: Concept of Sīla in Buddhism and Jainism: A Comparative Study.

Buddhism and Jainism are considered as the contemporary religions. Both the religions appreciate policy of non-violence. *Sīla* is an essential practice for the salvation in both the religions. Difference between these two religions in this regard is that Jainism is more extreme in practice than Buddhism.

In the Buddhist canon we can find the name of Nigaṇṭha Nāthaputta (Vardhamāna Mahāvīra). According to some Buddhist *sūtra*s we can find that Nigaṇṭha Nāthaputta is earlier and elder than the Buddha (*nigaṇṭho nātaputto saṅghī ceva gaṇi ca gaṇācariyo ca ñāto yasassī titthaṅkaro sādhusammato balujanassa rattaññu cirapabbajito addhagato vayoanuppatto—Sāmaññaphalasutta*). In this circumstance one can think that Buddhism has borrowed the techniques of Mahāvīra. Regarding that it can be said that both the religions are contemporary and may here influenced each other. Even though the appearance is similar among these religions but the atom is totally different. We intend have to find out the *sīla* and its function to obtain *nibbāna* and *kaivalya* in these two religions respectively.

I tried to collect the research material from original Pāli canon. VRI (Vipassanā Research Institute) *Tripiṭaka* C.D. was very helpful to me in this regard. *Visuddhimagga* and the Pāli commentaries were used to show the Theravāda idea of *sīla*. Prāk t and translated Jain texts were used for the research material of Jainism.

The first chapter of the work introduces the background of the main theme of the research and the second discusses the concept of *sīla* in Buddhism. The concept of *sīla* in Jainism is explained in the third and *sīla* as a pre-condition to enlightenment is the subject matter of the fourth chapter. Attention has been paid to the concept of *nibbāna* and *kaivalya* regarding this. The conclusion arrived at on the basis of foregoing analysis which forms the last chapter. It is my considered opinion that I have made a satisfactory contribution to the academic field through this book.

Acknowledgements

I owe my deep sense of gratitude and indebtedness to my supervisors: Dr. Ranjana Rani Singhal, Department of Buddhist Studies, Satyawati College (Eve) and Prof. L.P. Singh. I completed my work with their compassion advises and guidance.

I pay my special respect and deep reverence to the most Venerable Prof. Bhikshu Satyapala, Head of the Department of Buddhist Studies. He has not only inspired me in this work but also helped me in many ways, particularly as a research scholar of the Department of Buddhist Studies. I am greatly indebted to Prof. K.T.S. Sarao who has been with me in this work from the beginning to the end. I also thank all my teachers of the Department of Buddhist Studies. I owe a special debt of gratitude to scholars whose books and papers, etc., I have relied upon and have used in this work.

Particularly, I am highly grateful to my great teacher, late Ven. Pandit Dr. Medagoda Sumanatissa Nāyaka thero, the Chancellor of the University of Shri Jayawardhanapura and the chief incumbent of Sunethra Mahadevi Pirevena College at Pepiliyana, Sri Lanka.

I should be thankful to Prof. Sumanapala Galmangoda who advised me to choose this topic and also encouraged in various ways. I completed this research on the Commonwealth Scholarship, granted by Indian Council for Cultural Relations (ICCR). This scholarship was very helpful to carry on my research and I am glad to say that it was a great honour to me. Here I have to mention thankfully, Venerable Dr. Tumbulle Sri Silakkhandha Nāyaka thero, the Vice-Chancellor of Buddhist and Pāli University of Sri Lanka, who granted me leave, and Venerable Prof. Wegama Piyaratana and Venerable Dr. Ittademaliya Indasara thero who were the Vice-Chancellors at the time of my research work.

At the same time my great sympathy and gratitude goes to Late

Mr. Joe Neal of Australia who encouraged me in my studies and did lot of other things like computing, English, etc. It is true that I would not have been in this place if he would not have helped me.

Dr. Lalan Kumar Jha of the Department of Buddhist Studies was very helpful to find the research materials. Whatever I had problems not only regarding the research works but also in the other things he sorted out amicably. Librarian (DULS), Mr. Jha Ji (the assistant of our Department of Buddhist Studies), Jain Swami Dharmananda (Director, Adhyatmic Sadhana Kendra, a centre for spiritual training, Chhattarpur, India), Mr. Karamveer and his family (who took me all the places I wanted to visit to collect research material), are also worth mentioning. Friends who took care of me in this work in Sri Lanka, and who looked after my monastery and Sunethra Mahadevi University College, in absence of me are worthy of thanks. During this my stay in India Venerable Nakulugamuwe Wimalavansa and Venerable Pinwatte Anuruddha worked hard to maintain order in my monastery. Without their help I would not have finished this work in time.

At last but not least, I should be thankful to my parents and my closest friends who encouraged me in every step of progress. I wish to express my sincere gratitude to all those who supported to complete my studies during my stay in Delhi.

University of Delhi
December 2009

Medagoda Abhayatissa

List of Abbreviations

A.D.	—	Anno Domini
A.N.	—	*Aṅguttaranikāya*
Dept.	—	Departmental Publication
Dh.	—	*Dhammapada*
Dha.	—	*Dhammapadaṭṭhakathā*
Dhs.	—	*Dhammasaṅgaṇī*
DN.	—	*Dīghanikayā*
e.g.	—	(exempli gratia) for example
etc.	—	(etcetera) and the rest, and so on
i.e.	—	(id est) that is to say
Ibid.	—	Ibidem
Ja.	—	*Jātakapāli*
Jaa.	—	*Jātakaṭṭhakathā*
K.P.	—	*Khuddakapāṭha*
L.D.B.	—	*The Long Discourses of the Buddha*
Mahā	—	*Mahāvagga*
M.N.	—	*Majjhimanikāya*
P.B.E.	—	*The Perspective on Buddhist Ethics*
P.O.F.	—	*The Path of Freedom*
P.O.P.	—	*The Path of Purification*
P.T.S.	—	Pāli Text Society
Pattha.	—	*Paṭṭhānapāli*
SN.	—	*Saṁyuttanikāya*
S.P.	—	*Samantapāsādikā*
St.N.	—	*Suttanipāta*
Thera	—	*Theragāthāpāli*
V.R.I.	—	Vipassanā Research Institute
Vis.	—	Visuddhimagga
viz.	—	Videlicent—namely

Contents

1
Introduction

During different epochs of the history India has produced many saints in different parts. These saints earnestly tried to entangle the problems encountering the human beings and prescribe solutions for the well-being of them. Hardly, there is any country where so much emphasis is given to philosophical speculations. According to one scholar "Half the world moves on independent foundation which Hinduism supplied. China and Japan, Tibet and Siam, Burma and Ceylon look to India as their spiritual home."[1]

During sixth century B.C.E. two religions became prominent in India. These religions were Jainism and Buddhism. Both were contemporaries and held non-violence as a supreme virtue and also laid emphasis on *brahmacarya* (celibacy) and renuciation from the household life.[2]

Both the religions were kind towards animals and condemned animal sacrifies and preached kindness to all living being or creatures.[3] Above all both the systems laid emphasis on freedom from the cycle of birth and death rather than material prosperity and happiness.[4] Both the systems laid emphasis on supreme goal of *kaivalya* and *nibbāna*. Propounders of these two systems were the Mahāvīra and the Gautama Buddha. Both toiled hard and renounced their kingdoms and wandered in different parts of Bihar and U.P. and through meditation attained peace. For whole life they wandered and preached for well-being of living-being and both of them had several similarities and dissimilarities.

---

1. Cf. S. Radhakrishnan, *The Hindu View of Life,* p. 1.
2. Bhagcandra Jain Bhaskar, *Jainism in Buddhist Literature,* p. 1.
3. *Ibid.*
4. *Ibid.*

These similarities and common features compelled some earlier Western historians, for example Elphinston to propound the view that Jainism was "no more than offshoot of school of Buddhism which had very wide ramification in Asia and a much greater circle of followers in ancient India itself".[1] But all these opinions were changed when some more Western scholars like Jacobi and Hoernle studied the Jain and Buddhist traditions. They analysed minutely and proclaimed that the Jainism was an independent tradition and was at least two centuries older than Buddhism.[2] But with the progress of the studies it was found that both the traditions were contemporaries.

India and Buddhism

Some people become astonished to see phenomenal rise of Buddhism in India because when it arose it subsided Hinduism in Bengal, Assam, Bihar, Orissa and the other parts of India.[3]

Buddhism was a new idea for the society. It is a religion of kindness, humanity and equality. While the religion of the Vedas allowed animal sacrifice to propitiate the gods, Buddhism opposed sacrifice and wages merciless campaign against such practices.[4] The post-Vedic society was divided into four different categories, brāhmaṇas, kṣatriyas and vaiśyas enjoyed certain privileges in the society. Śūdras were the lowest in the order and had to bore the burden of other three upper castes. Brāhmaṇas enjoyed the higher position who were trained in complicated nature of sacrificial system.[5] According to *Kūṭadantasutta* of the *Dīghanikāya* tears were tickling from the eyes of śūdras for menial works.[6]

Another feature of great sociological significance of Buddhism was that it threw open the doors of organized religious life to women and men alike.[7]

Apart from this after initiation the Buddha used to instruct his

1. Bhagcandra Jain Bhaskar, *Jainism in Buddhist Literature,* p. 1.
2. *Op. cit.*, pp. 1-3.
3. Cf. "India and Buddhism", in P.V. Bapat, *2500 Years of Buddhism,* p. 1.
4. *Ibid.*
5. *Ibid.*
6. *Op. cit.*, pp. 1-2.
7. Cf. *Ibid.*, p. 3.

followers to go to different directions. Selfless band of workers were trained and dispersed the teachings of his master in different directions.

The Buddha took to small disputed points during his lifetime to be settled democratically. As the number of members increased in the Saṅgha office-bearers were appointed and laws were framed to regulate the life of monks and nuns. Thus it can be said that democratic methods were used to solve problems and decision of the Saṅgha was the final in regard to disciplinary matters.

Organized form of Saṅgha imparted education to the masses. It is education that changes lives of men or women even in the present life. Through Saṅgha mass education was imparted to local population.

Cause of Origin of Jainism and Buddhism

It is pertinent to note here that the primary cause of the rise of Jainism and Buddhism was the religious unrest in India in sixth century B.C.E. The complex rituals and sacrifices, highly philosophical nature of Upaniṣadic teachings and hegemony of priestly class, i.e. brāhmaṇas in all affairs of contemporary life led to discontentment among kṣatriyas and vaiśyas.

Besides the religious factor, social and economic factors also contributed to the rise of these two religions.

Several sects arose in the area of Middle Gangetic basin during the sixth century B.C.E. In the *Brahmajālasutta* of the *Dīghanikāya* the Buddha himself explains about sixty-two views[1]prevalent at His time.

The post-Vedic society was clearly divided into four *varṇa*s; brāhmaṇas, kṣatriyas, vaiśyas and śūdras. Each *varṇa* was assigned well-defined functions.[2] In this order śūdras had to serve all the upper three castes. Vaiśyas were engaged in agriculture, cattle rearing and trade. They were principal taxpayers.[3] Certainly, the *varṇa* divided society would have generated tensions.[4] The Kṣatriya's reaction against the domination of the priestly class, i.e.

1. *Dīghanikāya, Paṭhamo Bhāgo*, pp. 1-41.
2. R.S. Sharma, *Ancient India,* p. 60.
3. *Ibid.*
4. *Ibid.*

brāhmaṇas who claimed various privileges, was one of causes of the origin of new religions.[1]

Vardhamāna Mahāvīra, who founded Jainism and Gautama Buddha who founded Buddhism belonged to kṣatriya clan and disputed the authority of brāhmaṇas.[2] Before the time of the Buddha in the north-east India including the areas of western and eastern U.P. there were dense forests. After the time of Buddha these forests were cut and areas were developed for agriculture. Thick forest cover was depleting and areas became deforested. It was the time, when iron become prevalent in use. Use of iron on large scale resulted in deforestation. It utlimately gave rise to agriculture. Therefore, it is said that the near cause of the rise of these new religions was introduction of a new agriculture economy in north-eastern India.[3]

Other reasons of arising of these two religions are described as human settlements emergence of urban centres as. Several cities, e.g. Kauśāmbī near Allahabad, Kushinagar, Benares, Vaiśālī, Chirand (in Chapra district of Bihar) and Rājgīr and Patna, etc., can be seen.[4] All these cities arose in Bihar and modern Uttar Pradesh of India. The other reason for development of above two religions is said to be of generous donation from the vaiśyas communities. The first reason for this has been told as negation of *varṇa* system by both Buddhism and Jainism. The second reason is called as gospel of non-violence. It resulted in peaceful atmosphere that was conducive for development of commerce and trade. The third reason has been given by some authors as protest against Brāhmanical law book the Dharmasūtras that decried the moneylending trade of vaiśyas communities.[5]

Source Material for Buddhism

Source material for Buddhism regarding this topic is very vast. In the *Tripiṭaka* one can find teachings of the Buddha scattered at several places regarding morality (*sīla*). Among the three *piṭaka*s,

1. R.S. Sharma, *Ancient India,* p. 60.
2. *Ibid.*
3. *Ibid.*, pp. 60-61.
4. *Ibid.*, p. 60.
5. *Ancient India,* p. 62.

Vinaya Piṭaka itself means rules or regulations. At many places in the *Sutta Piṭaka* also one can find various explanations of morality (*sīla*). Even in the *Abhidhamma Piṭaka* mention of morality can be found.

In general the teachings of the Buddha provides lasting peace. If there is no peace within how can peace be reflected outside. If a person is not realizing peace in his own mind how can peace, will reflect by his deeds. When the peaceful activities reflected with one's action then only the society becomes peaceful. It is in this aspect that the world has recognized importance of the teachings of the Buddha and the UNO has started celebration of Vesākha day as peaceful day in the world. The last UNO day of Vesākha was celebrated by UNO in Vietnam from 13-17 May 2008.[1]

National Emblem of India

Remarkably the importance of Buddha's teachings can be seen in the National Emblem of India. In this emblem there is a horse in the left side and an ox on the other side of the plate. Between these two signs there is one wheel. All these are on an abacus. Above this abacus there are four lions with open mouths. In fact, in a figure there are only three lions which are visible.[2] Below the abacus one line is written, i.e. *satyameva jayate.* It is from *Muṇḍakopaniṣad.*[3] It means truth alone triumphs. The horse symbol, represent swiftness and the ox symbolized patience. The wheel symbolizes as motion.

At the same time there is *dharmacakra* on the national flag of India, which means moving forward, i.e. not to see behind but always yearning for development. There are twenty-four spokes in this wheel. This national emblem is a replica of lion capital of Sāranāth. In fact, it is part of Sāranāth pillar of the Aśoka the great. Here a question can be asked why there are only twenty-four spokes not more or less than twenty-four spokes in the wheel of the

---

1. Vesak Celebration and Conference Programme, United Nations day of Vesak Conference 2008 in Vietnam 13-17 May 2008, National Convention Centre, Hanoi, Published International Organizing Committee, Vietnam, 2008. Cover page.
2. *Sāmānya Jñāna Digdarśana,* p. 239A.
3. *Ibid.*

National Emblem and in National Flag of India. The answer is also supported from the tenets of Buddhism.

The answer of the above question can be given in two points based on Buddha's teachings. The first answer is there are twenty-four *paccaya* described in the *Paṭṭhāna,* the seventh book of the *Abhidhamma Piṭaka.*[1] Based on the twenty-four *paccaya* it is said that there are equal numbers of spoke in the wheel. The second answer can be again drawn from one of teachings of the Buddha. The theory of Dependent Origination is one of the most important teachings of the Buddha. Because once the Buddha told that one who understands my *dharma* understands *paṭiccasamuppāda* and who understands *paṭiccasamuppāda* understands my *dhamma* (*yo paṭiccasamuppādaṁ passati so dhammaṁ passati, yo dhammaṁ passati so paṭiccasamuppādaṁ passati*).[2] This teaching has twelve links which is known as *dvādaśanidāna.* When it is taken as in order (*anuloma*) and in reverse order (*paṭiloma*) it becomes twenty-four. Based on these two explanations it can be said that there are only twenty-four spokes in the wheel.

Now it is also important to note that why the lion capital of Sāranāth was taken as the National Emblem. Answer to this question can be given on the following lines. In the Indian sub-continent except one or two countries almost every country is associated with Buddhism. Where Islam is dominant there also Buddhism has different aspects like *mounds,* archaeological remains and Buddhist sites, etc. Even in the Southeast Asia Buddhism is prevalent in one way or the other. In coming days commercial activities of the nations will be developed in block. Blocks have been formed as Great Britain, Euro, Latin America, NATO. Nam, etc., for commercial as well as arms dealing, etc. Therefore, it can be said that the constituent assembly of India took a wise and foresighted decision in choosing national emblem and national flag.

Principles of Pañcasīla

The first prime minister of India had a very influential personality. He established cordial relations with his neighbours. To deal with other nations he started a five-point principles which became the

1. *Paṭṭhāna* (*Pṭṭha*), *Paccayaniddesa,* p. 16.
2. *M.N.*, *Mūlapaṇṇāsapāli, Mahātthipadopamasutta,* p. 251.

basis of Indian foreign policy. For this Paṇḍit Nehru signed a treaty with five-principles with Chau-en-Lai of China in 1954.[1] At that time Chau-en-Lai was a man of towering personality. Even in Sri Lanka there was a rule called *māghātaya* (do not kill). With the influence of Buddhism this rule took place at the time of King Devanāmpiyatissa.[2] As in the Asia these two countries were very populous and influential so they struck a deal which were guidelines of Indian foreign policy.

These principles are,

1. Mutual respect for territorial integrity and sovereignty
2. Non-aggression
3. Non-interference in each other's internal affairs
4. Equality and mutual benefit
5. Peaceful co-existence.

These five principles became very famous in the world. Many countries established their cordial relations with India. Principles of *pañcasīla* became basis for maintaining peace, stability, cordial bonds and friendly relations among the countries. Even in post-Independence period, it was Paṇḍit Nehru's thought and mental status that in the Wangdung Summit *pañcasīla* was signed. It is another matter that China invaded India in 1962 and occupied a vast land of tract of India.

Paṇḍit Nehru's *pañcaśīla* can be said influenced by five moral precepts (*pañcaśīla*) of Ten Percepts.[3] The very first precept is abstention from killing (*pāṇātīpātā vermaṇī*). The second precept is abstention from not to take what is not given to anyone (*adinnādānā vermaṇī*). In this way the third precept is called as *abrahmacariyā vermaṇī*, i.e. not to indulge in corrupt practices of flesh trade. The fourth precept is abstention from telling a lie (*musāvādā vermaṇī*). Somehow or the other influences of these precepts can be seen in the principles of *pañcaśīla* principle. Paṇḍit Nehru was very much influenced by Buddhism which is evident from his book, *The Discovery of India.*

---

1. R.C. Jain, *Upakāra Sāmānya Jñāna, Digdarśana Agara*-2, 2003, p. 383A.
2. E.W. Adhikaram, *Early History of Buddhism in Ceylon,* 1946.
3. *Khuddakapāṭha* (*KP*), pp. 5-7.

Source Material of Sīla

Morality (*sīla*) is such an important issue that can be found here and there in the *Tipiṭaka*. Even then the author will restrict himself on some definite place of the *Tipiṭaka*. At first morality (*sīla*) will be discussed from the *Khuddakapāṭha*. After that three kinds of *sīla*, i.e. *cūla sīla, majjhima sīla* and *mahā sīla* of the *Sāmaññaphalasutta* of *Dīghanikāya* will be discussed. It will be followed by morality of the householders. Morality described by Bhadanta Buddhaghoṣa will also be discussed in this work from the book *Visuddhimagga*. An effort will also be made to discuss merits and demerits of not following morality in this study. Other than different aspects of morality (*sīla*) discussed here its importance will also be shown for building solid foundation for living a household as well as the life of renunciation.

A short comparison will also be made regarding life and different aspect of teachings, etc., of the Mahāvīra and the Gautama Buddha in the last of this work. Here it seems necessary to give flow-chart of *Pāli Tipiṭaka*.

TIPIṬAKA

(1) *Vinaya*
(2) *Sutta*
(3) *Abhidhamma*

SUTTA PIṬAKA

(1)	(2)	(3)	(4)	(5)
Dīghanikāya	*Majjhima-nikāya*	*Saṃyutta-nikāya*	*Aṅguttara-nikāya*	*Khuddaka-nikāya*

Again *Khuddakanikāya* has 15 different texts. These are as follows:

Khuddakapāṭha
Dhammapada
Udāna
Itivuttaka

Suttanipāta
Vimānavatthu
Petavatthu
Theragāthā
Therīgāthā
Jātaka
Niddesa
Paṭisambhidāmagga
Apadāna
Buddhavaṃsa
Cariyāpiṭaka.

Abhidhamma Piṭaka

There are seven books in the *Abhidhamma Piṭaka*:

Dhammasaṅgaṇī
Vibhaṅga
Dhātukathā
Puggalapaññatti
Kathāvatthu
Yamaka
Paṭṭhāna.

In the Theravāda Buddhism various commentators wrote authentic books on different parts of the *Tipiṭaka*. Among the commentators Bhadanta Buddhaghoṣa, Ācariya Buddhadatta and Ācariya Dhammapāla are very important. Therefore, it seems necessary here to provide list of commentaries written by all these three great commentators (*aṭṭhakathākāra* or *aṭṭhakathācariya*).[1]

Commentaries of Bhadanta Buddhaghoṣa

Commentaries	*Parts of the Piṭaka*
Samantapāsadikā	Commentary on *Vinaya*
Kaṅkhāvitaraṇī	Commentary on *Pātimokkha*

1. Cf. Anomadarshi Barua, *Introduction to Pali,* Bhartiya Vidya Prakashan, Varanasi-1, Second revised and enlarged edition, 1977.

Sumaṅgalavilāsiṇī	Commentary on *Dīghanikāya*
Papañcasūdanī	Commentary on *Majjhima Nikāya*
Sāratthappakāsinī	Commentary on *Saṁyuttanikāya*
Manorathapūraṇī	Commentary on *Aṅguttaranikāya*
Paramatthajotikā	Commentary on *Khuddakapāṭha*
Attasālinī	Commentary on *Dhammasaṅgaṇī*
Sammohavinodinī	Commentary on *Vibhaṅga*
Pañcappakaraṇaṭṭhakathā	Commentary on *Dhātukathā-puggalapaññatti, Kathāvatthu, Yamaka* and *Paṭṭhāna*
Visuddhimagga	For the all *Tripiṭaka*
Dhammapadaṭṭhakathā	Commentary on *Dhammapada*
Jātakaṭṭhakathā	Commentary on *Jātaka*
Apadānaṭṭhakathā	Commentary on *Apadāna*

Commentaries by Ācariya Buddhadatta

Commentaries	*Parts of the Piṭaka*
Madhuratthavilāsinī	Commentary on *Buddhavaṁsa*
Vinayavinicchaya	Commentary on a compendium of the *Vinaya*
Abhidhammāvatāra	Commentary on a hand book of *Abhidhamma*
Uttaravinicchaya	A handbook of *Vinaya*
Jinālaṅkāra	A handbook on the *Pāramitā*

Commentaries by Ācariya Dhammapāla

Commentaries	*Parts of the Piṭaka*
Parmatthadīpanī	Commentary on *Udāna Itivuttaka, Vimānavatthu, Petavatthu, Theragāthā, Therigāthā* and *Cariyāpiṭaka*

Paramatthamañjusā	Commentary on *Visuddhimagga.*
Nettippakaraṇassa-atthasaṃvaṇṇanā	Commentary on *Nettippakaraṇa*
Saccasaṅkkepo	*Abhidhamma*

Here the readers can think what was the use of providing entire *Tipiṭaka* when only concerned portion of the work would have done the job. The main reason behind giving entire *Tipiṭaka* is that the present work consists of one chapter which furnishes comparison between Buddhism and Jainism. Therefore, the author felt that entire *Tipiṭaka* and Āgama of Jainism should be described in this work. At this juncture some explanations of the Jain texts are also needed.

Source Material for Jainism

Vardhamāna Mahāvīra was born in 540 B.C.E. in a village near Vaiśālī.[1] His father was the chief of a Jantrika clan and his mother was a Licchavī princess.

In the beginning Mahāvīra led the life of a householder but in the search of truth he renounced the world. At that time his age was 30. He kept on wandering for twelve years.[2] He was always on the move. He did not spend more than one day in a village and more than five days in a town.[3] While on the move he never changed his clothes for twelve years and attained *kaivalya* at the age of forty-two. He preached his teachings in the areas of Magadha, parts of Mithilā and Champā, etc.

In due course of time Mahāvīra asked his followers to lead a more austere life. On account of this, Jainism was divided into two sects, Śvetāmbaras or those who put on white dress, and Digambaras or those who keep themselves naked.[4]

Jainism recognized the existence of god but placed him below the *jina.* Jainism believed in soul and it did not condemn the *varṇa* system of the brāhmaṇas. Mahāvīra looked for human values even

1. *Ancient India*, p. 62.
2. *Ibid.*
3. *Ibid.*
4. *Ibid.*, p. 63.

in *cāṇḍāla*s or neglected people. He advocated that even lower caste people can attain liberation through pure and meritorious life. Full knowledge, action and liberation are considered as three gems or *ratna*s of Jainism.

Jainism spread to southern India. There were two main reasons for it. The first one is Mauryan king Candragupta Maurya (322-298 B.C.E.) became a Jain and left his throne and led the life of an ascetic. The second reason of spreading Jainism in Karataka may be ascribed to great famine that occurred near about 200 years after demise of Mahāvīra. The famine lasted for about 12 years and to protect their purity some Jainas went to the south under the leadership of Bhadrabāhu.[1] While some stayed at Magadha under the leadership of Sthūlabāhu. Here they started a council at Pāṭalīputra. According to their council there are forty-six canons.[2] These are as follows:

1. The twelve *aṅga*s:
   - (i) *Āyāraṅga*
   - (ii) *Sūyaḍāṅga*
   - (iii) *Thāṇāṅga*
   - (iv) *Samavāyāṅga*
   - (v) *Viyāhapaṇṇatti* (*Bhagavatī*)
   - (vi) *Nāyādhammakahāo*
   - (vii) *Uvāsagadasāo*
   - (viii) *Antagaḍadasāo*
   - (ix) *Anuttarovavaiyādasāo*
   - (x) *Pañhāvagarṇaṁ*
   - (xi) *Vivāgasūya*
   - (xii) *Diṭṭhivāya* (*vicchinna*)[3]
2. The twelve *Upaṅga*s:
   - (i) *Ovavāiya*
   - (ii) *Rāyapaseniya*
   - (iii) *Jīvābhigama*
   - (iv) *Pannavaṇā*
   - (v) *Shriyapaṇṇatti*
   - (vi) *Jambuddīvapaṇṇatti*

---

1 *Ancient India*, p. 62.

2. Jagdishchandra Jaina, *Prakrit Sāhitya Kā Itihāsa,* pp. 47-48.

3. *Ibid.*

(vii) *Chandapaṇṇatti*
(viii) *Niriyāvaliyāo*
(ix) *Kappavaḍaṃsigāo*
(x) *Pupphigāo*
(xi) *Pupphacūliao*
(xii) *Vaṇhidasāo.*

3. The ten *paiṇṇas:*
(i) *Causaraṇa*
(ii) *Āurapaccakkhāṇa*
(iii) *Mahāpaccakkahāṇa*
(iv) *Bhattapariṇṇā*
(v) *Taṇḍulaveyāliya*
(vi) *Saṃthāraga*
(vii) *Gacchāyāra*
(viii) *Gaṇivijjā*
(ix) *Deviṃdatthaya*[1]
(x) *Maraṇasamāhi.*[2]

4. The six *cheysuttas*:
(i) *Nisīha*
(ii) *Mahānisīha*
(iii) *Vavahāra*
(iv) *Dasasūyakkhaṅdha* of *Āyāradasāo*
(v) *Kappa* (*B hatkalpa*)
(vi) *Pañcakappa* or *Jīyakappa.*

5. The four *mūlasuttas*:
(i) *Uttarājjhayaṇa*
(ii) *Dasaveyāliya*
(iii) *Āvassaya*
(iv) *Piṇḍajijjutti* (*Ohanijjutti*).

6. The two *cūlikāsuttas*:
(i) *Nandī*
(ii) *Amuyogadāra.*

These are called Āgama literature.[3] The Digambraras refutes Āgama literature of Śvetāmbara.[4] For the scholars all these above-

1. At this place in *Jainism in Buddhist Literature* the word *Mahāpaccakkahāṇa* word is given, p. 35.
2. At this place in *Jainism in Buddhist Literature* is given *Viratthava,* p. 35.
3. Cf. *Prāk it Sāhitya Kā Itihāsa,* p. 47.
4. *Ibid.*

mentioned books are necessary ingredients of Prāk t literature. For the source material all these texts and some other texts provide a sound footing for writing on morality as discussed in Jain literature.

Coming to this point the author does not resist his temptation to provide commentarial literature of Jainism. To explain *aṅgas* and *upāṅgas* commentarial literature, i.e. *bhāṣya* and *cūrṇī* were also written.

Explanatory literature of Āgama is started with *niryukti.* The followeing *niryukti* books are mentioned in the Jain literature. It is said that these were written by Bhadrabāhu II.[1]

Āvasyaka-niryukti
Dasavaikālika-niryukti
Uttarādhyayana-niryukti
Ācārāṅga-niryukti
Sūtrak tāṅga-niryukti
Dasāsrataskandha-niryukti
V hatakalpa-niryukti
Vyahāra-niryukti
Piṇḍa-niryukti
Ogha-niryukti
Ṛṣibhāsita-niryukti.

All the above-mentioned books were written during the fifth and sixth century A.D. Apart from these, the commentarial literatures are as follows:[2]

Daśavaikālika-bhāṣya
Vyahāra-bhāṣya
V hatkalpa-bhāṣya
Nestītha-bhāṣya
Visesāvasyaka-bhāṣya (with by Jain *bhaelra samāsraman* in the seventh century A.D.)
Pañcakalpa-bhāṣya (by Dhammasena Guṇī during sixth century A.D.)

All these *niryuktis* and *bhāṣyas* are in verse. The language is *prāk t.* These are some literatures which are in the form sub-

1. *Jain Dharma and Darśana,* pp. 82-83.
2. *Ibid.*

commentary. The technical name given for these sub-commentaries are *cūrṇī*. The seventeen *cūrṇī*s are as follows:

Āvasyaka
Daśavaikālika
Nandī
Anuyogadvāra
Uttarādhyayana
Ācārańga
Sūtrak tańga
Niśītha
Vyavahāra
Dasāsruta-skandha
V hatkalpa
Jīvābhigama
Bhagavatī
Mahāniśītha
Jītakalpa
Pañcakalpa
Ogaha-niryukti.

The first eight from the above were written by Jinadāsa Mahatara. His period has been fixed around seventh century A.D. *Jitakalpa-cūrṇī* was written by Siddhasena Sūrī, during twelfth century A.D. The *V hatkalpa-cūrṇī* is ṭhe work of Pralamba Sūrī, while the others are anonymous.

As the commentaries of three great commentators had been given in the part of Buddhism so far the part of Jainism name of commentaries and their authors have been presented here.

Research Methodology

As is generally perceived, research work is composed of two words e.g., *re* and *search.* It means to search again or a careful investigation to re-understand or re-examining the facts or to search for new facts or to modify older ones in any branch of knowledge.[1] Here it seems logical to give some definitions of research.

1. Cf. *Research Methodology,* p. 1.

(a) Lundberg—"Research is sufficiently objective and systematic to make possible classification, generation and verification of the data observed".[1]
(b) Francis Rummel—"Research is a careful enquiry or examination to discover new information or relationships and to expand and to verify existing knowledge".[2]
(c) M.H. Gopal—"It is essentially a systematic inquiry seeking facts through objective verifiable methods in order to discover the relationship among them and to deduce from them broad principles or laws".[3]

Here we have given only three explanations of the word research. Even though it become a voluminous study, if we try to explain what is a research and research methodology.

Characteristics of Research

Research has several characteristics:

(a) Research is a scientific programme. It points out cause and effect. Research is directed towards solving a problem. Here in this work research will be directed to see how morality is explained in the light of above-mentioned texts.
(b) Research sometimes requires courage if the conclusions drawn are not popular and bring social disapproval.[4]
(c) In a research something is recorded and reported.
(d) Research can be said as a tool to solve human beings, problem. Thus purpose of research is to serve humanity.
(e) Research demands accurate investigation and description.

Classification of Research

Research is classified into two broad categories:

(a) Research is physical or natural sciences.
(b) Research in social or human sciences.

---

1. R.K. Verma and Gopal Verma, *Research Methodology* p. 2.
2. *Ibid.*
3. *Ibid.*
4. *Ibid.*

Here it is obvious that the purpose of this research (the present work) is to investigate something new in humanities.

Thus, it becomes imperative to say something about social science research because this work is related with social science and humanities. According to P.V. Young—

> "Social research seeks to find explanation to unexplained social phenomena, to clarify the doubtful and correct the misconceived facts of social life. Gathering knowledge for the sake of knowledge is termed as pure or basic research. Gathering knowledge that could aid in the betterment of human destiny is termed as applied or practical research. In reality no line of demarcation can be drawn between these two types of research. Each is dependent on the other for development and verification."[1]

At this point it is also necessary to say something about characteristics of social sciences research. There are various characteristics of social science research but important aspects are given here as it is not possible for giving in detailed account of these:

(i) Social science requires penetrating view and deep knowledge and careful investigation of the topic concerned.
(ii) Social science research is always objective. A researcher must not impose or take his own interest as it vitiates the universality of scientific position.
(iii) Social science research is dynamic and universal in nature, that is why what was true of past it is not necessary that it would become necessary in future too.

Now it is necessary to say something about method. Generally under social and economic research importance is given to the six main methods which are as follows:[2]

(1) Historical methods
(2) Case study method
(3) Experimental method
(4) Statistical method.

---

1. *Research Methodology*, p. 4.
2. *Ibid.*, p. 16.

The present work is based on historical method of study. Some aspect of the teaching of Mahāvīra and Buddha are compared. That is why this research will be obviously complying with a historical method. There are and there can be several definitions of historical method of research, but the most suitable definition seems that it is based on past reference.

There goes a good adage. If someone always dwells on past, he or she will loose one eye but if he or she never dwells on the past he or she will lose both of the eyes.

According to the observation of the P.V. Young—

> "The past if it can be located contained the key to the present, though today is different from the yesterday, it was shaped by yesterday. Today and yesterday will probably influence tomorrow."[1]

The present work mainly deals with the morality and duties performed by householders both in Buddhism and Jainism.

1. *Research Methodology*, p. 17.

2

Concept of Sīla in Buddhism

Sīla (morality) plays an important role in Buddhism. Whether it is Theravāda or Mahāyāna Buddhism *sīla* acts as precursor of a solid foundation of life. Whether it is concerned with the life of a recluse or a laity or a lay devotee *sīla* plays an important role for all of them.

In day-to-day life when we encounter an old man passing unwanted comment, our general opinion says that the old man is devoid of *sīla* or *sadācāra* (well conduct). In the same way if we see a teenager child doing something obvious to the society, then our attention immediately goes to his parents and suggests that parents of this child, has not taught the child the lessons of *sīla*. In this way if we see a group of boys travelling in a public transport like buses, trains or other means of transportation with unruly behaviour we immediately say that their parents have not trained them in the lessons of *sīla*.

Female members of a society are certainly thought to be very polite, well-cultured and bearer of moral behaviour. If a female is well-behaved, educated and followers of *sīla* that family naturally becomes cultured. Chances of becoming that family well-cultured family becomes very high. The Buddha used to talk about *hiri* and *ottappa* which is described as personal shame and social shame. The Buddha used to say that various persons do not do wrong activities due to these two entities. Some persons do not do bad activities minding personal shame. Others do not do bad or wrongful activities due to social shame. Therefore, the Buddha used to say that so long as *hiri* and *ottappa* are there, the society will exist. The moment these two terms disappear from society, that society will become meaningless. Buddhist literature used to give examples of girls from a noble family and prostitutes. It is used as *attagāravavasena pāpato jiguccanato kulavadhū viya hiri, paragārava vasena pāpato uttasanato vesiyā viya ottappaṁ.*[1]

While giving these examples, it further explains the way of walking, moving their hands and feet and other behaviours of the girls of a noble family. At the same time behaviours of prostitutes are very uncommon and indecent.

It means behaviour particularly sum total of behaviours of a person of his whole life. It plays an important role in shaping his or her life. Perhaps that is why the Buddha prescribed ten moral precepts for monks or nuns which is technically called as *daśa sikkhāpada*[2] (ten precepts), when they become members of the Saṅgha. These ten precepts are as follows:

(i) *Pāṇātipāta veramaṇī*
(ii) *Adinnādānā veramaṇī*
(iii) *Abrahmaccariyā veramaṇī*
(iv) *Musāvādā veramaṇī*
(v) *Surāmerayamajjappamāaṭṭhānā veramaṇī*
(vi) *Vikālabhojanā veramaṇī*
(vii) *Naccagītavāditavisūkadassanā veramaṇī*
(viii) *Mālāgandhavilepanadhāraṇamaṇḍanavibhūsanaṭṭhānā veramaṇī*
(ix) *Uccāsayanmahāsayanā veramaṇī*
(x) *Jātarūparajatapaṭiggahaṇā veramaṇī.*

Ten Precepts

Precept to Abstain from Killing (Pāṇātipātā veramaṇī)

It can be called as the first base of moral life.[3] Word *pāṇātipāta* has three parts. These are *pāṇā, ati* and *pāta. Pāṇā* refers to living being. *Ati* is a prefix which means quickly, rapidly.[4] *Pāta* can be defined as to fall, to make an end of anything or to destroy.[5] Therefore, *pāṇātipāta* can be explained as to destroy the life of any

---

1. *Abhiddhammatthavibhāvinīṭīkā* (V.R.I.) *Sobhana cetasika vaṇṇanā*, p. 105.
2. *KP*, pp. 5-7.
3. L.K. Jha, *Man and the Moral Base,* p. 28.
4. *Ibid.*
5. *Ibid.*

living being forcibly before its full span of time.[1] *Veramaṇī* can be expressed as abstention from or to abandon killing. Therefore, *pāṇātipāta veramaṇī* is the name of taking a vow so that a monk or a nun or a lay person takes it to remain aloof or abstain from the killing the life of a living being.

Here a question can be asked that what is killing and in this process what is destroyed? In general sense killing involves destruction of life. In specific sense it is *pāṇa-vadha* or *pāṇa-ghāta.*[2] *Pāṇa* refers here to man or living-being. Regarding killing it can be said that there is no permanent soul inside a being. A man is the composition of the five aggregates (*pañcakkhandhā*). These five aggregates generate a vital-force (*jīvitindriya*) that is destroyed when anything is killed.[3]

Precept of Not Taking Anything Which is Not Given (Adinnādānā veramaṇī)

The second precept is *adinnādānā veramaṇī. Adinnādānā* is the term made with *adinna* and *ādāna.* It has a negative meaning. It means not, absence of any thing, etc. It is a prefix having negative meaning. *Dinna* signifies the meaning of given, offered, presented, etc. *Ādāna* means to accept, to possess or to keep, etc. Combining all the three parts it becomes to take or to accept or to keep which is not given. In other words to take the things which has not been offered to anyone. Therefore, to take something becoming aware that it does not belong to him or her is *adinnādāna.*

Here it can be asked that in which condition the theft or stealing is materialized. The text provides five conditions in which theft is materilized.[4] These conditions are another's property,

---

1. *Kaṅkhāvitaraṇī aṭṭhakathā, Parājikākhaṇḍa,* p. 57.
   "*Tattha pāṇoti satto paramatthato jīvitindriyaṁ. Pāṇassa atipāto pāṇātipāto pāṇavadho pāṇa-ghāto pāṇātipāto, atthato ...vadhaka cetanā*" I owe this reference to L.K. Jha, *Man and the Moral Base,* p. 34.
2. *Kaṅkhāvitaraṇī aṭṭhakathā, Parājikākhaṇḍa,* p. 28.
3. *Ads* (V.R.I.), p. 176. I owe this reference to L.K. Jha, *Man and the Moral Base,* p. 34 "*Jīvanti tenāti jīvitaṁ, tadeva kammajarāparipālane adhipaccaya yogato indriyanti jīvitindriyaṁ*".
4. *A.S.* p. 81, *Khuddakapāṭha aṭṭakathā, Sikkhāpadavaṇṇanā, "paraparriggahitaṁ ca paraparriggahita saññī, theyyacittaṁ, upakkmo, tena haraṇaṁ ti."* I owe this reference to L.K. Jha, *Man and the Moral Base.*

awareness that a thing belongs to other, stealing mind, efforts for stealing and ultimately removal of that object as theft. All these acts are necessary for materialization of theft. If all the first four conditions are met and the last one is not materialized then stealing will not take place. In the same way there are several ways or means of stealing the things of others. Likewise there can be several kinds of thefts. In the *Samantapāsādikā* there are twenty-five kinds of theft.[1] Since the text *Samantapāsādikā* is an ancient text of fifth century A.D. so the author of the text has mentioned twenty-five kinds which were prevalent at that time. In modern times the theft can be divided into some more kinds as the things and situation both have changed.

Precept of abstaining from Unchastity (Abrahmaccariyā veramaṇī)

The third precept is *abrahmaccariyā veramaṇī*. It can be divided in two parts, e.g., *a* and *brahmaccariya*. *A* means absence or to be away from. *Brahmaccariya* means noble or high. Joining both the parts meaning becomes to be away from unchastity (celibacy). Its meaning is unchastity. That is to say that one has not become involved in various kinds of unlawful sexual activities.

The text mentions about ten types of unmarried women and the same types of married women who should not be treated as the source of sexual satisfaction.[2] These women have been mentioned in the context that no body has any right to approach them for sexual desire. In the same way another text describes ten kinds of married women whom a person has no right to entertain for sexual desire.[3]

Here it is important to mention that other term for *abrahmaccariya* is also used. That term is *kāmesumicchācāra*. *Kāmesumicchācāra* means wrong conduct in sexual pleasures. Such kind of conduct is liable to be blamed. *Abrahmaccariya* term is used in the context of monks and nuns. While *kāmesumicchācāra* is used in the sense of householders. A monk or a nun has to refrain completely from unchastity. They have not to think even in the

1. *S.P.* I (Nal.) 298.
2. *A.S.*, p. 81, I owe this reference to L.K. Jha, *Man and the Moral Base*.
3. *Ads.* II (V.S.V.), p. 536.

consciousness about this low activity. A householder is advised to remain satisfied with his wife only. He has not to develop in his consciousness sexual deeds other than his wife. It is in this context the above two terms are used.

Precept of Abstaining from the False Speech (Musāvāda veramaṇī)

Musāvāda is a constituted of *musā* and *vāda. Musā* signifies the meaning of untrue or false. *Vāda* refers to the meaning of speech, talk, discussion and theory, etc. It means to talk or speech which is not true. This morality refers to the meaning of refraining from the false speech. *Veramaṇī* refers to abstaining from the false speech. Now it is necessary here to define how it is materialized. The text presents four conditions which are necessary for materialization of false speech.[1] After dealing with four conditions, ways of different kinds of false speech are necessary. There are various ways like *kuhanā, lapanā, nemittikatā, nippesikatā* and *lābhenalābhaṃ-nijigiṃsanatā*, etc.

Kuhanā means deceitful pretensions (to attainments). *Lapanā* means cheating others with attracting or more attracting statements. *Nemittikatā* refers to subtle insinuation by signs and indication (for gain). *Nippesikatā* refers to means of attracting the people by using the expressions of criticisms, rebuking, anger and charge of an imaginary faults. *Lābhenalābhaṃ-nijigiṃsanatā* is a wrong way of earning livelihood by giving up smaller gains in the hope of getting a bigger one.

Pharusā vāca (harsh, unkind, fierce, savage, rough, rugged, severe and cruel words), *pisuṇāvāca* (tale bearing) and *samphappalāpa* (meaningless, frivolous talk or idle talk) are also included in this *musāvādā* term.

---

1. *A.S.*, p. 82. "*Tassa cattāro sambhārā honti-atathaṁ vatthum, visaṃvādanacottaṁ, tajjo vāyāmo, parassa tattha vijānanaṁ ti*". I owe this reference to L.K. Jha, *Man and the Moral Base,* p. 56.

Precept of Abstaining from Taking Liquor That Causes Intoxication (Surāmerayamajjappamādaṭṭhānā veramaṇī)

Surā is referred as arrack or spurious liquor. *Meraya* signifies wine (intoxicating liquor, spirit, rum, arrack or strong drink). *Majja* refers to intoxicating drinks which makes a man senseless or mad. *Pamādaṭṭhānā* throws light on situation where a man drinks finding an opportunity.

At the time of the Buddha different kinds of *surā* or *meraya* were used by the people. One can find five kinds of *surā* in a text.[1] Like *surā, meraya* has also been described as having five kinds.[2] Now it can be asked here that in which conditions or factors drinking of *surā* or *meraya* is materilized. Significantly the text has given four conditions in which drinking of *surā* and *meraya* are materialized.[3] It can be added here that all these conditions are mentioned during the fourth century A.D. One may differ regarding all these conditions and can add some more conditions in the light of present times.

There are various results of abstaining from arrack and wine. One who abstains bears sound memory. He never becomes nervous if he has not any serious disease. He is always in the possession of knowledge and remains mindful and careful. A man can place himself in the higher state in society by not taking arrack, wine or intoxicating drinks. It is the highest gain or auspices sign.[4]

Precept of Abstaining from Eating at the Wrong Time (Vikālabhojanā veramaṇī)

Vikālabhojana is broken as *vi, kāla* and *bhojana. Vi* is a prefix which has negative or special meaning. *Kāla* refers to time or period. *Bhojana* means to eat food, partake or to take meal. In this

---

1. *P.J.*, p. 25 "*Surā ti pañca surā-piṭṭhasurā, pūvasurā, odanasurā, kiṇṇapakkhattā, sambhārasaṃyuttā cā ti*". I owe this reference to L.K. Jha, *Man and the Moral Base,* p. 61.
2. *S.P.* II (Nal.), p. 884.
3. *P.J.*, p. 31.
4. *St.N.* (V.R.I.), p. 122:
   Ārati virati papa, majjapānā ca saṃyamo|
   Appamādo ca dhammesu, etaṁ maṅgaamuttamaṁ||

way *vikālabhojana* means to eat at prohibited time or wrong time. This precept was given by the Buddha regarding *sattarasa* monks in the Rājagaha. People gave them food after taking bath when these monks went for begging alms in the city. After begging these monks went to a garden and ate the alms in prohibited time. This matter was reported to the Buddha. The Buddha made a law—"whosoever a monk eat any kind of food at prohibited time is responsible for *pācittiya*".[1]

It is necessary here to say something about the materialization of *vikālabhojana.* The text prescribes four conditions in which *vikālabhojana* can be materialized.[2] At the same time it is also necessary to discuss the kinds of food which have been debarred. These foods are *odanaṁ* (boiled rice), *kummāsaṁ* (a preparation of barley), *macchaṁ* (fish), *māṁsaṁ* (meat) and *sattuṁ* (prepared by gram).[3] Whatever of these food monks or nuns take in afternoon is breaking that *sīla* or rule.

Precept of Abstaining from Vulgur Shows of Dancing, Singing and Music (Naccagītavāditavisūkadassanā veramaṇī)

This precept deals with various kinds of dances and dramas, etc. *Nacca* means dance. Dance includes various kinds whether accompanies by musical instruments or it is simply movements of the body. *Gīta* refers to singing. It means mere singing or singing that is associated with instruments. These instruments can be drum, cymbal, *vīṇā* or flute, etc. *Vādita* refers to music. *Visūkadassana* means acrobatic shows which are performed in club, theatres, and fairs and on some occasions. Thus it can be said to see or to watch dancing, singing, music and acrobatic shows without carrying the norm of the Dharma and the society is *naccagītavādita-visūkadassanā.*[4]

---

1. *Pācittiyapāli* (V.R.I), p. 118: "*Yo pana bhikkhū vikāle khādanīyaṁ va bhojanīyaṁ vā khādeyya vā bhuñjeyya vā pācittiyaṁ".*
2. *P.J.*, p. 36 "*Vikālabhojanassa cattār aṅgāni-vikālo, yāvakālakaṁ, ajjhoharaṇaṁ, anumatta-katā".* I owe this reference to L.K. Jha, *Man and the Moral Base,* p. 66.
3. *S.P.* (Nal.) II, pp. 842-43.
4. *S.V.* (V.R.I.), p. 5. I owe this reference to L.K. Jha, *Man and the Moral Base,* p. 70.

If someone visit the show with desire then it is a transgression. In case of walking, standing and visiting a place if a show comes into his way then it is not a transgression.

Precept of Abstaining from the Use of Garlands, Scents, Unguents and Wearing Finery (Mālā-gandhavilepana-dhāraṇamaṇḍana-vibhūsanaṭṭhānā veramaṇī)

Mālā signifies garland. It also refers to any kind of preparation or decoration made by garlands of flowers. *Gandha* refers to a substance, from which sweet fragrance comes out. *Vilepana* refers about different kinds of lotions, ointments, cosmetics or creams, etc. *Dhāraṇa* means to wear, to use or to make these things part of life by using these things daily. *Maṇḍana* refers to finery or ornaments or adornment, etc. Garlands, sweet fragrance, ointments and adornments, etc., are not for *maṇḍana* (good looking) and *vibhūṣaṇa* (beautiful appearance or adornment).

From the very beginning garlands have been used in Indian society. It has been used in man's various acts like worship, honouring a person, for adornment of to decorate stage, etc. There are various ways of making garlands. And the text has prescribed six methods of its preparation.[1] In the same way the text prescribes different kinds of fashions of dressing the lock of hair. Six kinds of ways of weaving wreaths of flowers can be seen in the text.[2] For handsome looking or beautiful appearance a man has to use various things for adornment of hairs. In this context the dialogues between child Nāgasena and Thera Rohana can be cited. Like a curious child Nāgasena asks him about his shaved hair. Then Thera Rohaṇa says there are sixteen impediments (*soḍasapaḷibodha*) for higher life.[3] The discussion goes like this that a man has to adorn his hair in different ways. When there is no hair people cry or lament for black hairs.

---

1. *S.P.* (Nal.) II, p. 621: "*Gandhanādisu sabbāpi ca pupphavikatiyo veditabbāganthaṁ, gopphimaṁ, vedhimam, veṭhimaṁ pūrimaṁ, vāyimaṁ ti*". I owe this reference to L.K. Jha, *Man and the Moral Base,* p. 74.
2. *Ibid*., p. 620.
3. *Milindapañha* (V.R.I.), p. 10.

Precept of Abstaining form Using High and Large Beds (Uccāsayanamahāsayanā veramaṇī)

Uccāsayana refers to sleeping on abnormally high or lofty beds. Heights of these beds are higher than standard height. *Mahāsayana* means the beds which are very broad. Such type of beds which are exceedingly high and extremely broad are not to be used by a monk.

Once a monk named Upananda was living in Sāvatthi. He was in the habit of sleeping on the high and lofty beds. One day the Buddha visited that *vihāra*. Upananda showed him his bed. On seeing his bed the Buddha made a rule, "A monk should make a new bed which is eight fingers in height with the fingers of Sugata (the Buddha). Whosoever cuts it after transgressing its height is responsible for *pācittiya*."[1]

There are various kinds of couches which should be avoided by a monk or nun. Even in the case of householders too, those who have simple life, high or lofty beds are not advisable.

Precept of Abstaining from Accepting Gold and Silver (Jātarūparajatapaṭiggahaṇā veramaṇī)

It is the last precept, *jātarūpa* generally signifies gold. It is now wide open that gold is used for monetary-medium and for ornaments too, etc. It is non-rustic and malleable element. Due to its wide use it is called noble metal (*suvaṇṇa*). *Rajata* means silver. While gold is yellow, silver is white. Silver is lustrous precious metal which is used chiefly in production of coins. It can be said here that the term *jātarūparajata* refers to alloys made of gold and silver. *Paṭiggahaṇā* refers to acceptance of gold and silver or their alloys in any form.

Thus goes the story about framing of law by Gautama Buddha. There was a monk named Upananda. He was in the habit of receiving alms from the certain houses of Rājagaha. One day meat was prepared in that house. Some portion of the meat was put aside for the monk. But a child of that house ate the meat preserved for Upananda. After that he accepted gold and went to the market to eat

---

1. *Pācittiyapāli* (V.R.I.), p. 222: *"Navaṁ pana bhikkunā mañcaṁ vā Pīṭhaṁ vā kārayamānema atthaṁgulapādakaṁ kāretabbaṁ sugataṅgulena aññatra heṭṭhimāya aṭaniya, taṁ atikkāmayato chedanakaṁ pācittiyaṁ".*

meat. This matter was reported to the Buddha and he framed a law—"If any monk accepts gold and silver or causes to accept other or accept accumulated property, he is defaulter of *nissaggiya pācittiya.*"[1]

Other than this *sīla* discussion of three kinds of *sīla* are found in the *Sāmaññaphalasutta* of the *Dīghanikāya.*[2] *Cūḷasīla* (small morality), *Majjhimasīla* (medium morality) and *Mahāsīla* (Greater Morality). Under *cūḷasīla* such types of profession or actions have been elaborated which cannot be considered good or pious. These profession or livelihood can be said easily immoral. In the section *majjhimasīla* such types of livelihood or professions have been included which can be said immoral or moral by thinking and by directing the mind towards the profession little bit more. Under *mahāsīla* such types of professions are included which need greater efforts than the *majjhimasīla* in determining moral and immoral.

Small Morality (Cūḷasīla)

When the King Ajātasattu asked the Buddha about a monk who is endowed with the small morality (*cūḷasīla*), the Buddha replied in the following way.

By abandoning the killing of living being, abstaining from taking what is not given to him, forsaking false speech, abandoning malicious speech, etc., he lives a life of morality. A monk speaks what is blameless and pleasing to the ears, etc. He abandons idle chatter and speaks at the right time what is correct and is according to the point of the *dhamma* and discipline. A monk refrains from destroying different kinds of seeds, seedlings, etc. He eats only one time and refrains from eating at night and improper times. He avoids watching dancing, singing, music and contronist shows. He abstains from using garlands, perfumes, cosmetics, ornaments and adornments. He refrains himself from using high and lofty beds and bedsteads. He avoids accepting gold and silver. He avoids accepting raw grain or raw flesh. He does not accept young girl, women, slave either male or female, sheep, goats, cocks and pigs, elephants,

1. *Pācittiyapāti* (V.R.I.), p. 215: "*Yo pana bhikkhū jātarūparajataṁ uggaṇheyya va uggaṇhā peyya vā upanikkhittaṁ vā sādiyeyya, nissaggiyaṁ pācittiyaṃ*".
2. *DN.* (Depart.), pp. 41-75.

horse, mare, fields and plots. He avoids buying and selling things under false weights and measures, from bribery and corruptions, highway robbery, etc. This is small morality.[1]

Middle Section on Morality (Majjhimasīla)

After elaboration of the morality of the small section, the Buddha replies to King Ajātasattu on the morality on the middle section. The Buddha starts this morality with the destruction seeds or seedlings. According to him a monk should refrain himself from destruction of different kinds of seeds that are propagated from roots, from stems, from joints, from cuttings, from seeds, etc. A monk should remain aloof from the addiction of enjoyment of stored up goods as food, drink, clothing, carriages, beds, perfumes and meat, etc. This is also known as *sīla.* The Buddha also advises the king that a monk should remain abstained from watching different kinds of shows, e.g. fight of elephants, buffaloes, bulls, goats, rams, cocks and quilt, etc., and different kinds of fightings, e.g. with staffs, boxing and military reviews, etc.

Other kinds of professions mentioned by the Buddha and presented in the text are addiction to such games and idle pursuits as eight or ten row chess (*aṭṭhapādaṁ-dasapādaṁ*), chess in the year, hopscotch, spillikins, dicing, hitting sticks, hand pictures, ball games, blowing through toy pipes, guessing letters (*akkharikāro*), etc. All these are called by the Buddha as morality of the middle section.[2]

The discussion goes on and the Buddha says that one who eats food having received from faithful and are addicted to high or wide beds, couches adorned with animal figures (*goṇakaṁ cittakaṁ*), embroidered with gems or without, elephants, horse or chariot-rugs, Couches with awnings or red cushions at both ends (*ubhato lohitakūpadhānaṁ*), etc.[3]

In the same way the Buddha elaborates that a monk after eating the food given by *upāsaka*s or *upāsikā*s should not addict to different kinds of self-adornment and embellishment as rubbing the body with perfumes, massaging, bathing in scented water,

1. *L.D.B.*, pp. 68-89.
2. *Ibid.*, p. 70.
3. *Ibid.*

shampooing, using mirrors, ointments, garland, scents, headbands, turbans, yak-tail fans, long fringed white robes, etc.[1] These are also expressed under morality of the middle section (*majjhimasīla*).

Refraining from such types of discussion in which unedifying conversation about the king (*rājakathā*), robbers (*corakathā*), minister (*mahāmattkathā*), towards speculation about land and sea and talks about birds and other beings and non-beings (*tiracchānakathā*), etc., are also the part of the morality of the middle section described by the Buddha and explained by the text.[2]

The Buddha also explains some trivial talks like—

> "How could you understand this doctrine and discipline, your way is all wrong, mine is right, I am consistent—you are not, you said what should have been used first "go on save your doctrine—get out of that if you can." These talks are also the part of discussion of morality of the middle section.[3]

At last Buddha says that deception, labours, hinting, belittling and all ways to make further gains (*lābhena lābhaṁ nijigiṃsanatā*), etc., are also the part of morality of the middle section.[4]

Supreme Section on Morality (Mahāsīla)

Under this *sīla* the Buddha says that base arts or wrong means of livelihood as palmistry, divining by signs, portents, dreams, body-marks, mouse-gnawing, and fire oblations should not be entertained. Oblations from a ladle, of husks, rice-powder, rice-grains, ghee or oil, from the mouth or of blood, reading the finger tips, house and garland-lore, skill in charms, ghost lore, earth-house lore, snake-lore, poison-lore, rat-lore, bird-lore, foretelling a person's lifespan, charms against arrows, knowledge of animal's cries, etc. An ascetic should refrain from such kinds of wrong livelihood.[5]

Further the Buddha says about the various other base arts like judging the marks of gems, sticks, clothes, swords, spears, arrows, weapons, women, men, boys, girls, male and female slaves, etc. The list also includes marks and their readings on animals like elephants,

1. *L.D.B.*, p. 70
2. *Ibid.*
3. *Ibid.*, p. 71.
4. *Ibid.*,
5. *Ibid.*, pp. 71-72.

buffaloes, bulls, cows, goats, ram and cocks, etc. He advises that a monk should refrain from all these false livelihood.[1]

In this list the Buddha also enlists prediction of base arts like this king will make advance, another king will retreat, our kings will win and other king will lose, etc. The list also includes prediction about eclipses of moon, the sun, etc., and prediction of bad rainfall, a good or bad harvest, epidemic, etc. The Buddha also suggests that a monk should not indulge in giving and taking in marriage, engagements and divorces, using spells to bind the tongue, binding the jaw, etc.[2]

The Buddha makes an end to the list with wrong means of livelihood by appearing the *deva*s and redeeming vows to them, making earth-house spells, causing virility or impotence, preparing and consecrating building sites, giving rituals, ring signs and bathing, making sacrifies, giving emetics, purges, etc.[3] He advises monks to remain abstain from such kind of activities.

Sīla: As Duties of a Person

Disāpūjanasīla

After discussion on morality of three sections a brief discussion is presented here on *disāpūjanasīla.* This *sīla* was elaborated by the Buddha to a householder named 'Sigāla' at the shelter of *kalaṅdaka.* In this *sutta*[4] the Buddha prescribed various things for the householders, different causes of destruction of properties, properties of friend and foe and duties of householders and worshipping of different directions, etc.

'Sigāla', the householder was worshipping the different directions without knowing its meaning. The Buddha instructed him to know the meaning of different directions and also elaborated him the use of worshipping the different directions. He advised him that the father and mother are represented by the eastern direction (*mātāpitā disā pubbā*). The teacher is assigned by the southern direction (*ācariyā dakkhinā disā*). Sons, daughters and wives are

1. *L.D.B.*, p. 72.
2. *Ibid.*
3. *Ibid.*, pp. 71-72.
4. *Pāli Sāhitya Kā Itihāsa,* p. 192.

denoted by the western direction (*puttadārā disā pacchā*). Friends and other relatives are represented by the north direction (*mittāmaccā ca uttarā*). Below is denoted by servants and workers (*dāsakammakarā heṭṭhā*). While zenith is represented by brāhmaṇas and *samaṇa* (*uddhṁ samana brāhmanā*).[1] The householder should claim his duties to these six directions. Then only his life becomes auspicious, sacred and he can achieve the goals that he wishes.

Maṅgala Sīla

The *sīla* was delivered by the Buddha to a deity in the Jetavanavihāra at Sāvatthī. One deity appeared during the night and asked the Buddha about good omen or the highest good. The Buddha elaborated about several good things which he considered good for a man. It is in the verse form and thirty-eight points are explained.[2] They are as follows:

> Not associating with fools,
> But cultivating association with wise man,
> Worshipping those who are worthy to be worshipped,
> Dwelling in a pleasant locality,
> To have done good deeds in the past,
> To have life with right desires,
> To possess great learning,
> Skill,
> Well-learnt in discipline,
> Well-spoken words,
> Waiting on one's mother and father,
> Protecting children and wife,
> A quite calling,
> Giving alms,
> Living religiously,
> Protecting relatives,
> Blameless deeds,
> Ceasing and abstaining from sin,
> Refraining from intoxicating drink,
> Perseverance in the Dhamma,

---

1. *P.B.E.*, p. 69.
2. *KP.*, pp. 13-18.

Reverence,
Humanity,
Contentment,
Gratitude,
The hearing of the Dhamma at due seasons,
Patience,
Pleasant speech,
Seeing Samanas,
Religious conversation at due seasons,
Penance,
Chastity,
Discernment of the Noble Truths,
The realization of Nibbāna,
He whose mind is not shaken, touched by the things of the world,
Free from sorrows,
Free from defilement,
Secure,
Invincible.

By observing these good omens position of any person does not come down. The Buddha advocates the deity by saying that one should learn various arts and skills, should obey parents, should speak soothing words. A man should abstain from killing living beings and telling a lie, etc. The man should associate with wise persons and to honour those who are worthy. To live at these places which are calm and quiet and according to their choices. People should also collect good *kamma* of their past deeds.

The Buddha advocates people to obey and respect other persons, to remain contented with one's own belongings, to become grateful to the service rendered to them by others. The Buddha advises people to remain calm in the worldly affairs. At the end of the *sutta* the Buddha says that if people follow these omens they are benefited and do not loose anything in their lives.

General Precepts for Householders and Monks

As there are ten precepts for monks or nuns so there are ten precepts for householders' too. It is mere co-incidence that both the numbers are ten. Ten precepts (*dasasikkāpada*) are partially meant for householders too. It has already been elaborated in preceding pages so there is no use of repeating it. Here it can be said that these precepts are for the welfare of householder but monks and nuns can take inspiration from these and preach it to householders. These are: *dāna, sīla, bhāvanā, apacāyana, veyyāvacca, pattidāna, pattānumodanā, dhammassavana, dhammadesanā* and *ditthi-uju-kamma.*[1] Now each term needs some explanation.

Dāna

This term has a great significance in Buddhism. It is widely used term which means giving something to another person; offering and parting away some income from one's own earning for charity, etc. It should be a regular affair in which some portion of one's earnings be parted with for needy or charity work with friendliness. But this offering should not be for show or with haughtiness. *Dāna* has been explained in the following way. "There is scriptural sanction of offering to the extent of one-fourth of one's earnings (*catudhā vibhajate loke*)."[2] Again this offering should be of three kinds, e.g. like a slave, like a good friend and like a master. Slave offering is equated with the offerings of poor people. Friendly offering has been told to give sizeable income of one's property with pleasant feelings. The master-like offering is narrated as giving entire property for the greater causes, e.g. upliftment of downtrodden, education or for construction of monastery, etc. *Dāna* is the first part of *pāramitā*s too. There are many stories about giving offerings in ancient literature. In the *Petavatthu* it is said that offerings given by relatives on the *paṭthaviloka* (on the earth) liberates *peta*s (spirits) as *peta*s do not eat grains.[3]

Sīla

This is the second precept for the householders. In a way the present work is totally related with *sīla* (morality). Here the meaning of *sīla*

1. *K.N.* I, p. 4. Here I owe it to the *Perspective of Buddhist Ethics,* Mahesh Tiwary, pp. 67-69.
2. *Perspective on Buddhist Ethics*, p. 68.
3. *Tirokuddasutta, Khuddakapātha* (V.R.I.), p. 15: "*ito dinnena yāpenti, petā kalakatā tahiṁ*".

is explained in a different sense. It means that one should have unshakable faith or unwavering confidence in morality. This vow should be kept for the whole life. Therefore, the word *ajjataggepāṇupetaṁ* in Pāli is used for the taking this vow. That means one is taking this vow today and will follow it for one's whole life. The benefit of this precept is in the beginning (*ādi kaḷyāṇaṁ*), in the middle (*majjhe kaḷyāṇaṁ*) and at the end (*pariyosāṇaṁ kalyāṇaṁ*) too.

Bhāvanā

It is special term which is used for meditation. Concentration of mind is achieved by this process. Pāli literature talks about forty kinds of objects of meditation (*kammaṭṭhāna*). These objects prescribe the object of meditation. It is directed by a teacher who is called as a well-wisher friend (*kalyāṇamitta*). About him it is said that he should be dearly loved. Highly esteemed, venerated, ability of well counselling, a patent listener, capable of delivering oneself to useless end. All these are in a verse from which is as follows:

> *Piyo ca garubhāvaniyo-vattā ca vacanakkhamo*।
> *Gambhīrañ ca kathaṁ kattā-nocaṭṭhāne niyojaye*।।[1]

Pattidāna

Patti means the fruit of meritorious deeds. It is said that fruits of meritorious deeds are necessary for births in higher plain or *bhūmi*s. Meritorious deeds provide sound basis for rebirth. By meritorious deeds a person rejoices not only in this birth but also in future birth too. There are different kinds of virtuous, pious or meritorious deeds. One of the most important meritorious deeds is to remove suffering of others or to bail out a person from his pain or suffering. The offering is called as *pattidāna*.

---

1. *Vis.*, p. 79.

Pattānumodanā

It is the name of receiving something particularly offering of merit (*patti*) from someone with pure consciousness and with clear heart. Sometimes it is seen that a person does receive any dhammic offering easily. Therefore, it can be said that *pattānumodanā* refers to receive offerings with love or loving kindness.

Veyyāvacca

Service to humanity or any other service should be through pleasant feelings. It is generally seen that some persons donate something in compulsion. In some of the cases an elderly person prevails upon someone, and he resents to do charity, etc. Charity or offerings should not be in binding or compelling condition. Rather it should be from the core of the heart. One's inner feelings should be such that service and other things should be his habit. It is known as *veyyāvacca.*

Apacāyana

It is the name of general behaviour of a person. Other nearer term in English can be as etiquette. How a person should behave with another person, how he should take care of an old man and his parents, etc., can be explained under this. It is said in the *Dhammapada* that who is in the habit of obeying and serving elderly people his four qualities increase, e.g. age, fame, happiness and his bodily strength. It is as follows:

> *Abhivādanasīlissa-niccaṁ vaddhāpacāyino*|
> *Cattaro dhammā vaddhanti-ayu vaṇṇo sukhaṁ balaṁ*||[1]

Desanā

Dhamma is what the Buddha taught. *Desanā* means to preach. Combining this means to share the teachings of Buddha. An eloquent householder can also deliver dhammic talks. And also he

1. *Dh.* (V.R.I.), v. 109, p. 102.

can collect that merit what is accumulated by the monks who are preaching the *dhamma.*

Dhammasavanā

It is not very easy that a man would attend dhammic talk. There are various persons who attend various other gatherings but not the gatherings where any eloquent speaker is talking on any aspect of the *dhamma.* In the *Maṅgalasutta* it said that a person should pay respect to humble, to remain satisfied with what one possesses, to remember or become grateful towards the favour received from others and to listen to the religious discourses (delivered on the truth or reality) time to time. This is called as the best auspicious omen (blessings):

> *Gāravo ca nivāto ca—santuṭṭhī ca kataññutā*।
> *kālena dhammasavanaṁ—etaṁ maṅgalamuttamaṁ*।।[1]

Buddha advises the people there is no mother or father without *dhamma. Dhamma* is the only salvation. So one who is full with vice, he should listen, keep in mind and behave in *dhamma.*[2]

Diṭṭhi ujukamma

Diṭṭhi signifies wrong views (62 kinds in the *Brahmajālasutta*).[3] *Uju* means to make straight. Therefore, to make the mind free from the false views is called *diṭṭhi ujukamma.* It is said in the *Dhammapada* that an intelligent person should make his views (mind) straight as a bow-maker straights the arrows:

> *Phandanaṁ capalaṁ cittaṁ—durakhaṁ dunnivārayaṁ*
> *ujuṁ karoti medhāviṁusukāro va tejanaṁ*[4]

This is called as *diṭṭisaṁvara.* There are four kinds of

1. *KP.*, p. 17.
2. *Rasavāhinī Dhammasoṇḍakavatthu* (V.R.I.), v. 10: *dhammameva suṇissāmī—dhamme me ramatī mano...*
3. *DN, Sīakkhandavagga, Brahmajālasutta* (V.R.I.), pp. 1-41.
4. *Dh, Cittavagga* (V.R.I.), v. 33, p. 17.

attachments (*upādāna*). They are *kāma upādāna, attavāda upādāna, sīlabbata upādāna, avijjā upādāna* and *diṭṭhi upādāna*. Here *diṭṭhi upādāna* means attachment to the wrong views. The Buddha's advise not to attach with the views (*diṭṭhi*) but to be with correct vision (*dassana*).[1]

Vinaya Rules of Saṅgha Community

The detailed description of the *vinaya* rules, prescribed by the Buddha to regulate to life of monks and nuns in the *Vinayapiṭaka*, occupies an important place in the Buddhist tradition. These are meant to regulate their lives and direct them to make the threefold activities pure. A path is prescribed and the goal is stated. These also help them to realize the goal of salvation—(*nibbāna*) by gradual training (*anupubbasikkhā*), peforming the course of actions (*anupubbairiyā*), and following the noble path gradually (*anupubbapaṭipadā*). The Buddha as a practical thinker has prescribed *vinaya* rules with full consideration of the beings. The rules are to guide the life as a whole for them. There is a big section of *vinaya* rules, specially meant for restraining and regulating the physical, vocal and mental activities of the monks and nuns for leading monastic life. The *vinaya* rules have been collected and put in the *Vinayapiṭaka*. The monks and nuns are required to follow these sincerely for the benefit of their spiritual upbringing. These are not commandments of the Buddha like those that are found in Christianity and Judaic religions of the West. These have been prescribed for the benefit of those leading the spiritual life. However, they are free to follow them. There is no compulsion or coercion for following these rules.

The words, monks and nuns are the English rendering of the two terms *bhikkhu* and *bhikkhunī*. The word *bhikkhu* is defined as one who *begs for alms*.[2] Thus the literal meaning of the word *bhikkhu* is a beggar of alms. It is only one aspect of the meaning of the term. He is not a beggar in true sense of the term. He is a man of sacrifice. He has no belongings. He does not preserve anything for himself but lives on alms given by others. In this way, for the sake of preserving his life, he wanders and begs for food from door to

---

1. *St. N., Mettasutta* (V.R.I.), p. 107.
2. *Vibhaṅga, jhānavibhaṅga, mātikā, "bhikkhatīti bhikkhū"* (V.R.I.), p. 275.

door. In doing so, he does not beg for making accumulation but to keep the body fit for leading a holy life (*yāpanāya vihiṁsūparatiyā, brahmaccariyānuggahāya*)[1]. In this sense he desires a roof to sustain his life. It is offered a *bhikkhu* in the sense of honour. This offering is worthy and a *bhikkhu* also becomes worth of offerings and worship. The word has another sense too. He does not become *bhikkhu,* only by begging alms, but he abandons the householders' life and takes up the life of the recluse for some higher gains.[2] He understands that man is under the flare of sufferings. He takes birth and dies again and again and experiences various kinds of sufferings in this process. It is not a happy situation. As such, he takes up the life of a recluse to come out of such sufferings. It is only possible through the realization of *nibbāna.* Therefore, a *bhaikkhu* is he, who sees fear in repeated existence and makes an endeavour to attain *nibbāna.* In this background the definition of the *bhikkhu* has been given as who sees fear in the world is the *bhikkhu.*[3]

Saṅgha literally means group. With the meaning of one who kills perfectly this word is used. What does he kill? The answer is all the defilements. Thus it refers to a group of persons who join together after eliminating their defilements. The monks live together after destroying all the distinctions of caste, creed, etc., for the realization of the higher truth, that is *nibbāna.* Such persons, associated together in complete harmony stand for the Saṅgha. The text describes a monk as one who is a *samaṇa* who possesses the following characteristics:

The *bhikkhu* is the one who controls his mouth, who speaks wisely and calmly, who teaches the meaning of the truth, and his words are sweet.[4] A *bhikkhu* though receives a little from other does not despise him. His life is pure and he is not slothful. A *bhikkhu* is full of delight, is happy in the following doctrine of the Buddha, attains final bliss (*nibbāna*) consisting in the cessation of natural inclinations. In this way, the *bhikkhu* is a pious man engaged in

---

1. *Vis., Paccavekkhanā, Paccayasannissitasīla* (V.R.I.), vol. I, pp. 29-30.
2. *SN, Sagāthakavagga, Bhikkakasutta* (V.R.I.), p. 212: *na tena bhikhū hoti yavatā bhikkhate pare*
3. *Vis.* (V.R.I.), p. 4.
4. *Dh., Bhikkuvagga* (V.R.I.) v. 362, p. 58: *hatthasaññato pādasaññato... tamāhu bhikkuṁ.*

purgation of his life higher realizations. The number of such persons gradually increases in time and soon appears collectively as *bhikkhusaṅgha.* It may be a fact that in the beginning it was a small group but due to the noble activities of the monks it developed as a highly regarded and well organized order of the recluse. There were also other teachers who were contemporary of the Buddha but the textual facts clearly bear the evidence that the Buddhist order of Saṅgha become more popular among the people.

It is seen that there should be some reasons due to which the institutions like *pabbajjā, upasampadā, vassāvāsa, pātimokkha-uddesa, adhikaraṇa, adhikaraṇasamatha*, etc., came into being. The specific code of discipline prescribed by the Buddha to direct them towards the noble path may be considered as one reason for the rapid expansion of the *bhikkhusaṅgha.* The other reasons may be the Buddha's personal experience of religious life, his birth in the royal clan of Śākyas in Kapilavatthu, etc. His charismatic personality, noble character full of compassion, self-sacrifice, spiritual attainments combined together to create the great personage at whose feet as a spiritual preceptor thousands of people willingly gathered for the proper advice for realization of the truth by which emancipation from the sāṁsāric bonds is possible.[1]

Another fact that can be seen in this context is the method of teaching by the Buddha. He gave sermons to his disciples without keeping any thing secret as a close fist (*ācariyamuṭṭhi*). Everything was open to all. The method of his teachings runs as follows:

He used to give sermons on giving (*dānakathā*), sermons on virtues (*sīlakathā*), sermons on evil effects of the fivefold sense-desires (*kāmānaṁ ādinavaṁ*), sermons on the vulgarity of sensual pleasure (*okāraṁ saṅkilesaṁ*), discourses on the benefits of renunciation of the life of the sensual pleasures (*nekkhamme ca ānisaṁsā*), and when the mind of the receiver is receptive (*muducitta*), and devoid of hindrances (*vinīvaraṇacitta*) then there is the discourse on four truths.

Yet another reason can also be ascribed. The early members of the Order (Saṅgha) were not merely devout but also were renowned for their noble behaviours. The Buddha gave his sermons inspiring them for making right efforts. Thus, following the path with

1. *DN., Pāṭhikavagga, Udumbarikasutta* (V.R.I.), p. 40.

devotion, thy soon realized the truth. Thereafter, he instructed them to go forth for the benefit of all, for the happiness of all and in this way gave equal opportunity to every person from the highest position of king to the lowest scavenger to achieve the state of perfect peace and tranquillity. This method of instruction by the Buddha was appreciated by all. Most of the followers of other paths found that the method of the Buddha was the most acceptable and worthy. The realization was also very easy and quick. It is for this reason, that many people joined the Order to have the flavour of Dhamma in a short time.

With the passage of time of number of those who entered the order of monks increased, problems connected with their monastic life became more acute. The Buddha gradually prescribed rules for regulating their everyday life in order to achieve purity. In this regard, the Buddha established initially the *pabbajjā* institution.[1] The *upasampadā* institution (the higher ordination) also went on together with the *pabbajjā* for sometime, till the Saṅgha was in a formative state.

The term *pabbajjā* is interpreted in many ways. In general sense, it means coming out. In its technical sense, it is the act of abandoning the household life and taking the life of a recluse. The term *pabbajjā* in subsequent texts is described as he who has destroyed his defilements. He is also called *samaṇa brāhmaṇa* and *bhikkhu* as well as *pabbajjitā,* because he abandons all evils and worldly pleasures.[2]

It is seen that as soon as a man joins the Saṅgha, he becomes equal in all respects, irrespective of caste, creed, etc., with other members of the order, in the same way as the great rivers lose their names and identities, as soon as they flow into the great ocean.[3]

According to the *Mahāvagga,* the first performance of the ordination *pabbajjā* and higher ordination *upasampadā* for the *aññākondañña* mendicant, was accompanied by the Buddha calling him as "come forth oh monk – (*ehi bhikkhu*)". The other four mendicants namely, Bhaddiya, Vappa, Mahānāma, Assajjī were also ordained by calling them as "Come forth oh Monks (*etha*

1. *Mahā., Mahākhandhaka* (V.R.I.), p. 25.
2. *Dh. Daṇḍavagga* (V.R.I.), v. 142, p. 31.
3. *SN, Mahāvaggapāli, Maggasaṁyutta, Dutiyapācīnaninnasutta* (V.R.I.), p. 378.

bhikkhavo) in the same way.[1]

As the member of monks increased the Buddha had to frame different laws to regulate their lives. In this process he advocated 227 rule for monks and 311 rules for nuns. These rules are called *pātimokkha, Pātimokkha* means liberation of everyone. Every practitioner has to liberate himself in accordance with all these rules. These rules for the monks are as follows:[2]

Pātimokkha-saṃvarasīla

Pārājikā dhammā	=	04
Saṅghādisesā dhammā	=	13
Aniyatā dhammā	=	02
Nissaggiyā-pācittiyā dhamma	=	30
Pācittiyā dhamma	=	92
Pāṭidesanīyā dhammā	=	04
Sekhiyā dhammā	=	75
Adhikaraṇasamathā dhammā	=	07
Total	=	227

All these were recited on the day of *uposatha* and the confession was made by guilty monks. This *sīla* should be undertaken by faith.

Here it is necessary to present brief explanation of all these *dhammas*.

Pārājikā dhammā — under the section such types of activities are mentioned by which a monk is no longer the member of the Saṅgha. These are sexual intercourse (*methunadhamma*), stealing (*adinnādāna*), to praise death and killing a human being and to boast oneself as great as a knower of a supermundane state, etc.

Saṅghādisesā dhammā —These are such types of offences for which only Saṅgha can prescribe punishment or can exonerate the charge levelled against any particular monk. About this one author says that "It is so called because the imposition of the punishment as also the absolution from these offences require the presence of the Buddhist Saṅgha at the beginning as well as at the end."[3]

1. *Mahā, Mahākhandhaka* (V.RI.), p. 16.
2. *P.S.I.*, p. 388.
3. *P.L.L.*, p. 364.

Aniyatā dhammā – The meaning of the term *aniyata* is itself uncertain. Here nature and its punishment are not clear. As for example if a monk talks with a woman on a public place or in seclusion, charge levelled against the monk by a noble female devotee depends on how the monk accepts it.

Nissaggiyā-pācittiyā dhammā —Thirty kinds of rules under this section are divided into three sub-sections, e.g. robe (*cīvara*), wool (*loma*) and bowl (*patta*). For such types of punishment monks have to confess the guilt and after accepting punishment things are also forfeited.

Pācittiyā dhammā — Ninety-two offences are mentioned under this section. If a monk accepts his fault then he is exonerated from the charge and set free. Under this section there are some rules which are above temporal boundary. As for example—eating at only one time for a monk, to remain vigilant at the time of instructing a nun and to protect monk-hood, etc.

Pāṭidesaniyā dhammā —There are four rules under this section. These rules are related to the food given to monks. *Pāṭidesanā* means to ask for forgiveness.[1]

Sekhiyā dhammā —There are seventy-five rules under this section. These rules are related to external behaviour and discipline. How a monk should wear his robes, how he should move his hands and feet, how he should go for alms-round and how he should behave with a householder, etc., are described in this section.[2]

Adhikaraṇasamathā dhammā — All the seven rules under this section are related to pacifying of quarrel or dissent inside the Saṅgha. When there was a discontent among the members of the Saṅgha all these rules played important role in normalization of the situation.

Abstainment from the so-called prohibited behaviours and to obey the *pātimokkha* rules is called *pātimokkhasaṁvara sīla.*

Indriyasaṃvarasila

Indriya refers to six internal senses known as *salāyatana.* In the same way there are six external senses (*ālambana*). These are as follows:

1. L.K. Jha, *Man and the Moral Base,* p. 93.
2. *P.S.I.*, p. 396; I owe this reference to L.K. Jha, *Man and the Moral Base,* p. 93.

Six internal senses	*Six external objects*
cakkhu (eye)	*rūpa* (visible object)
sota (ear)	*sadda* (audible object)
ghāṇa (nose)	*gandha* (odourous object)
jihvā (tongue)	*rasa* (sapid object)
kāyā (body)	*poṭṭhabba* (tangible object)
mana (mind)	*dhamma* (ideational object)

Six internal senses are also called as sense doors. When anything come into the contact of the internal sense there develops a reflection in the mind. This reflection of object in the mind through different senses happens through different processes, e.g. *bhavaṅga, calana, javana, manodvārāvajjana, sampaṭicchana, santīraṇa* and *votthapana*, etc.[1]

A question can be asked here that what *saṁvara* is. Restrainment of indulgence in any kind of sense object is called *saṁvara.*[2] In day-to-day life we see a common example. If a beautiful woman passes through nearby some people start analysing different parts of her body. Some people always relish her picture in their mind. It is called act of indulgences. It is not proper. One should restrain in such kind of indulgences. It can be termed as restrainment of indulgence through eye-door. In the same way one should consider restrainment through the rest of the sense doors. This restrainment of indulgence through sense-doors is called *indriya-saṃvara.* A fine explanation of this can be seen in the *Dīghanikāya*.[3]

With suitable examples this *sīla* has been explained by Bhadanta Buddhaghoṣa in his text the *Visuddhimagga.* Referring *indriya-saṃvara* he says that the eye does not see a visible object because it has no mind. The mind does not see because it has no eye. When there is impingement of door and object he sees by means of the consciousness that has eye sensitivity as its physical

1. *A Manual of Abhidhamma,* pp. 231-32.
2. L.K. Jha, *Man and the Moral Base,* p. 87.
3. *DN.* (Deptt.), p. 62: *Kathaṁ ca mahārāja bhikkhu indriyesu guttadvāro hoti. Idha mahārāja bhikkhu cakkhunā rūpaṁ disvā na nimittaggāhī hoti nānubyañjanaggāhī.*

basis.[1] It is followed by an example of an elder *mahātissa* who was on begging alms for food from *cetiyapabbata* of Anurādhapura. A wife having quarrelled with her husband set out for the house of her relatives. She was at low mind and went on laughing. The elder saw her teeth. Realizing the perception of foulness the elder attained the *arahanta*hood. It is found in the text as follows:

> "He saw the bones that were her teeth, and kept in mind the first perception, and standing on that very spot the elder became an *arahant.*"[2]

The story proceeds like this. Her husband followed her. He came into contact of the elder and asked him about his wife. The elder answered him which is presented by the text in the following verse form:

> "Whether it was a man or woman, that went by I noticed not,
> but only that on this high road, there goes a group of bones."[3]

In this way a mendicant should understand the *indriya-saṃvara sīla* or restraint or subjugation of the senses.

Ājīvapārisuddhisīla

This is about right kind of livelihood. *Ājīva* refers to profession, occupation or way of eking out one's livelihood. *Pārisuddhi* means sanctity or purity of the way of earning livelihood. *Ājīvapārisuddhisīla* has been explained in the *Visuddhimagga*[4]. The explanation goes with the following terms *kuhanā, lapanā, nemittikatā, nippesikatā* and *lābhena lābhaṁ nijigimsanatā*, etc.

Kuhanā: It is explained as "deceitful appearance of a saint by matted hair, putting ash on the body and developing an attractive posture sitting on a cross road".[5] It is something like exilaration of

1. *P.O.P.*, p. 23.
2. *Ibid.* and *Vis.*, p. 19:
   Tassa dantaṭṭhikaṁ disvā pubbasaññaṁ anussari |
   Tattheva so ṭhito thero arahattaṁ apāpuṇī ||
3. *P.O.P.*, p. 23 and *Vis.* p. 19:
   Nābhijānāmi ittī vā, puriso vā ito gato |
   Api ca aṭṭhisaṅghāto, gacchatesa mahāpathe ||
4. *Vis.*, pp. 20-21.
5. *Perspective on Buddhist Ethics* p. 71.

one's position too. In the *Visuddhimagga* it is mentioned as scheming, grimacing, or disposing posing, composing, etc., for gain or fulfil wishes.[1]

Lapanā: It is a certain kind of profession which is gained by using attractive words in a mysterious way and thereby entrapping the passerby.[2] It is such a profession in which livelihood is earned by which a monk or a householder engages others in talking, persuading, suggesting, flattering or fondling, etc.[3] Everyone does not possess such quality. It is such quality which some clever persons or monk does with cheating mind.

Nemittikatā: In this method a sign is made in the body of a man and interpretation is in a charming and in a convincing way. This is highlighting a sign with highly resounding mystic expressions.[4] In the translation of the *Visuddhimagga* it is explained as "Hinting a sign or an indication, indirect talk some reference, etc., are given to others in the hope of receiving something then it is called *nemittikatā*".[5]

Nippesikatā: It is expressed as "means of attracting the people by using the expressions of criticism, rebuking, anger, charge for an imaginary faults, etc."[6] In the translation of the *Visuddhimagga* it is explained as "it is the name of abusing others, disparaging, reproaching, snubbing and backbiting, etc., with a hope to gain something."[7]

Lābhenalābhaṁ nijigiṃsanatā: It is a particular way of earning livelihood in which something is given to someone with the anticipation that more income will come in this process. A fine example is seen in the translation of the *Visuddhimagga.*[8] One monk was on alms round. He started from the beginning of a village where he got rice-pudding. He went on. At the end of the village he narrated about getting rice-pudding in the anticipation of getting more valuable or delicious thing from the householder.

1. *P.O.P.*, p. 25 and *Vis.*, pp. 20-21.
2. *P.B.E.*, p. 71.
3. *P.O.P.*, p. 25.
4. *P.B.E.*, p. 71.
5. *P.O.P.*, p. 25.
6. *P.B.E.*, p. 71.
7. *P.O.P.*, p. 26.
8. *Ibid.*, p. 31.

Tuḷākūṭa (deceiving people by means of balance and having some gain thereby), *kaṃsakūṭa* (under weight dealing) and *mānakūṭa* (wrong use of balance), etc., are also called wrong means of livelihood.[1]

Paccayasannissitasīla

Paccayasannissita sīla means the morality relating to four kinds of requisites, e.g. robe (*cīvara*), food (*piṇḍapāta*), dwelling place (*senāsana*) and medicine (*gilānapaccaya-bhesajja-parikkhāra*).[2] At the time of using all the things mentioned above a monk should remain aware. A monk uses robe only for protection from heat, cold, gadflies and only for the purpose of concealment of private parts.[3] In the same way a monk should eat food only for survival of the body. Regarding *senāsana* he uses it only from the protection of heat, cold and from some creepers and animals. He takes medicine becoming aware that by this he will get rid of disease and would be protected from hurtful feelings. For medicine a monk generally used urine, ghee, oil, etc.[4]

In the *Visuddhimagga* a good simile about the requisite is given. There was a novice who was nephew of the Thera Saṅgharakkhita. He was a voracious eater. His preceptor advised him to become mindful in eating and other requisites. Following the instruction the novice acted accordingly and attained *arahat*hood. He became satisfied and proclaimed that all his cankers have faded away. This is his last birth. He would not take birth again.[5] In this way all the above-mentioned *sīla* should be understood. According to the Buddhist point of view *sīla* is not a practice which is given by some body to another. It is clear that *sīla* is someone's own observation. *Samādiyāmi* means "I observe". If someone observes any precept he is responsible for that. Protecting *sīla* or breaking of it is his own wish. Purification or seduce is one's own problem. No body can purify another.[6]

---

1. *P.B.E.*, p. 72.
2. L.K. Jha, *Man and the Moral Base.* p. 94.
3. *P.O.P.*, p. 31.
4. *Vis.*, p. 37.
5. *P.O.P.*, p. 45.
6. *Dh*, *Attavagga,* (V.R.I.), v. 165, p. 34.

Sīla is important until the decay (*sīlaṁ yāva jarā sādhu*).[1] The education without *sīla* is useless (*sīlenānupetassa sutenatthā nvijjatī*).[2] Those who are not good in behaviour and not well cultured their education is useless (*yāvadeva anatthāya ñattaṁ bālassa jāyatī*).[3] These two occurrences are very important when we look at the current society. Those who are engaged in the criminal activities may be well educated people, but not well in moral behaviour. Even highly qualified doctors are found stealing the organs of human body for money. So education without well cultivated mind is not useful. That's why Buddha said *apadāna sobhinī paññā* (wisdom is beautiful if there is good behaviour).[4]

Generally young people think that *sīla* is to be practised by the old people. But the Buddha spreach morality for the young (*yuvā care brahmaccariyaṁ*).[5] It is convenient to behave in *sīla* as a young than the old those who cannot control themselves. When one's five faculties are weak and uncontrolled, how can they behave in *dhamma*.[6] That's why Buddha proclaimed *sīla* is essential until old age (*sīlaṁ yāva jarā sādhu*).[7]

There is no such a smell like *sīla* which is blowing with lower wind and upper wind equally.[8] The fragrance of sandal or other perfume is spreading in limited area. But smell of *sīla* is going up to the haven.[9] There is a story related to this in *Dhammapa datthakathā* the commentary of the *Dhammapada*[10] as *Mahākassapatthera Piṇḍapāta Dinnavatthu*.

There are five kinds of benefits to a person who protect or behave on the *sīla*. These are as follows:

(i) He obtains a huge wealth (*mahantaṁ bhogakhandaṁ*

---

1. *SN, Devatāsaṃyutta Jarāsutta,* (V.R.I.), p. 42.
2. *Ja, Pñcakanipāta, Sīlavīmansa Jātaka,* (V.R.I.), p. 108.
3. *Dh, Bālavagga,* (V.R.I.), v. 72 p. 22.
4. *AN, Tikanipāta, Bālavagga, Lakkhaṇasausuta,* (V.R.I.), p. 124.
5. *Ja., Mahānipāta, Mūgapakkhajātaka,* (V.R.I.), j. 538.
6. *Dh., Yamakavagga, Cakkhupālatheravatthu,* (V.R.I.), Vol. I:
   Jarājajjaritā honti, hatthapādā anassavā ǀ
   Yassa so vihatatthāmo, kathaṁ dhammaṁ carissati ǁ
7. *SN., Devatāsamyutta, Jarāsuttaṁ,* (V.R.I.), p. 42.
8. *Vis., Sīlaniddesa,* (V.R.I.) p. 10.
9. *Dh., Pupphavagga,* (V.R.I.), v. 56, p. 20.
10. *Dha., Mahākassapattherapiṇḍapātadinnavatthu,* (V.R.I.) vol. I.

adhigaccati).

(ii) He possess a good fame (*kaḷyāno kittissaddo abbhuggaccati*).

(iii) He attends any meeting without hesitation (*visāradova parisaṁ upasaṅkamati*).

(iv) He passes away without a complicated mind (*asammūḷho kālaṅkaroti*).

(v) He will be born in haven after his demise (*kāyassa bhedā paraṁ maraṇā sugatiṁ saggaṁ lokaṁ uppajjati*).[1]

In this sense *sīla* is very beneficial for the both this life and the next. In *Visuddhimagga* of Buddhaghoṣa, we can see a lot of questions (*pañhakamma*) about *sīla*. That would be very helpful to understand what is *sīla* in its exact meaning. There it is said.

Visuddhimagga Explanation on Sīla

1. What is *sīla* ? (*kiṁ sīlaṁ*?)
2. What is the meaning of *sīla*? (*kenaṭṭhena sīlaṁ*?)
3. What are the characteristics, function and outcome of *sīla*? (*kānasa lakkhaṇa rasa paccupaṭṭhāna padaṭṭānāni*?)
4. What are the benefits of *sīla*? (*kimānisaṃsaṁ sīlaṁ*?)
5. What are the classification of *sīla*? (*katividhaṁ sīlaṁ*?)
6. How can *sīla* be seduced? (*ko cassa saṅkileso*?)
7. How it can be purified? (*kiṁ vodānaṁ*?)

What is Sīla?

Abstaning from killing, etc., and fulfilment of good behaviour is *sīla*. There it is mentioned in this category that *cetanāsīla, cetasikasīla, saṃvarasīla, pātimokkhasaṃvarasīla, satisaṃvarasīla, ñāṇasaṃvarasīla, khantisaṃvarasīla, viriyasaṃvarasīla, avītikkamasīla*, etc. There are the moral behaviours which are coming in various aspects.

1. *DN, Mahāparinibbānasutta, Sīlānisaṃsakathā,* (V.R.I.), pp. 67-68.

What is the meaning of sīla ?

There are mainly two points in this context.

He observes *sīla* to have good actions (*samādānaṁ vā kāya kammānaṁ*)

It becomes the base of wholesome (*upadhāraṇaṁ vā kusalānaṁ dhammānaṁ*)

Here first line describes how a stop or abstention (*virati*) and second is the base of other good activities (*samādāna*).

What are the characteristics, function and outcome of sīla?

Lakkhaṇa

Well behaviour of the bodily action, etc., and base of the meritorious deeds are the characteristics of *sīla*.

Rasa

Eradicating violence and establishing well behaviour is called as *rasa*.

> *Dussīlya viddhansanatā – anavajja guṇo tathā* |
> *Kicca sampatti atthena – raso nāma pavuccati* ||[1]

Paccupaṭṭhāna

Paccupaṭṭhāna shows how we can understand *sīla*. With the purification we can see it (*soceyya paccupaṭṭhānam*). If someone's physical, vocal and mental behaviour is purified then we can understand that he dwells with *sīla*.

Padaṭṭhāna

The *padaṭṭhāna* or base of *sīla* is called as *hiri* and *ottappa*. (*ottappaṁ ca hiriṁ ceva, padaṭṭānanti vaṇṇitaṁ*). *Hiri* means shame to do unwholesome deeds. *Ottappa* means fear to do

1. *Vis.*, *Sīlaniddesa,* vol. 1, (V.R.I.), p. 1.

unwholesome act.[1] Fear of sinning, shrinking from sin, having a tender conscience, conscientiousness is called *ottappa*.

A person who has *hiri* is just like a horse of superior breed (*asso bhadro*). A horse coming from good family is shy of sentence or punishment. So it does not make even one mistake twice. Likewise the man should be shameful to do unwholesome deeds. That is called *hiri*. *Ottappa* means fear. That is also the fear to do *akusala* or uwholesome actions. There are four categories of *ottappa*:

(i) *Attānuvādabhaya* (fear of self-blame)
(ii) *Prānuvādabhaya* (fear of public blame)
(iii) *Daṇḍabhaya* (fear of punishments)
(iv) *Duggatibhaya* (fear of hell or state of punishment).[2]

At the beginning of this chapter the author has mentioned some more details of the *hiri* and *ottappa* as the base of *sīla*. Therefore, it is not being explained here in detail.

What are the benefits of the sīla?

In this chapter the benefits of the *sīla* is discussed in detail. It is said that there are endless benefits of *sīla* (*avippaṭisārādi anekapaṭi lābhānisaṃso*)[3].

What are the classification of sīla?

There are various kinds of classifications of *sīla*. *Sīla* is onefold according to the point of well behaviour.[4] It has two facets in different ways as given below:

cāritta	*vāritta*
kālapariyanta	*āpānakoṭika*
ābhisamācarika	*ādibrahmacariyaka*

1. *DN.*, *Pāthikavaggapāli*, *Saṅgītisutta*, (V.R.I.), p. 188.
2. AN., *Catukkanipāta*, *Bhayavagga*, *Attānuvādabhayasuttaṁ*, (V.R.I.), pp. 139-40.
3. *Vis.*, *Sīlaniddesa*, (V.R.I.), p. 9.
4. Vis., *Sīlaniddesa*, (V.R.I.), p. 9: *sīlanaṁ lakkhanaṁ tassa*.

virati	*avirati*
nissita	*anissita*
sapariyanta	*apariyanta*
lokiya	*lokuttara*

It is threefold,

hīna	*majjhima*	*paṇīta*
attādhipateyya	*lokādhipateyya*	*dhammāddhipateyya*
parāmaṭṭha	*aparāmaṭṭha*	*paṭippassaddhi*
visuddha	*avisuddha*	*vematika*
sekha	*asekha*	*nevasekha nāsekha.*

It is of fourfold,

hānabhāgiya	*ṭhitibhāgiya*	*visesabhāgiya*	*nibbrdabhāgiya*
bhikkhu	*bhikkhunī*	*anupasampanna*	*gahaṭṭha*
pakati	*ācāra*	*dhamatā*	*pubbahetuka*
pātimokkhasaṃ-vara	*indriyasaṃvara*	*ājivapārisuddhi*	*paccayasnnisita*

There all are the categories of *sīla* mentioned according to their characteristics. In *Visuddhimagga* mainly *catupārisuddhisīla* is discussed in details but the rest is very brief. There is no doubt as a secondary work to the Dhamma, *Visuddhimagga* is the best collection of the material on *sīla* in Buddhism.

Those who are protecting *sīla* should do it like she bird *kikī* which protects its eggs carefully. Same way he should protect *sīla* as a yak who protects its own tail. Further, he should be able to protect *sīla* as mother who has only one child and a person who has only one eye.[1]

Buddha himself proclaimed that there is no fragrance like *sīla*. It blows in all the directions equally.

---

1. *Sumaṅgalavilāsinī, Sīlakhandavagga Atthakathā, Cūlasīlavaṇṇanā,* (V.R.I.), Vol. I.

Sīlagandhasamo gandho kuto nāma bhavissati ।
Yo saman anuvātañca paṭi vātañca vāyati ।।[1]

In all the major categories of Buddhism we can find *sīla*. At the ten fulfilment of the qualities of enlightenment (*dasapāramitā*) second limb is *sīla*.[2] We can see in the *Jātakapāli* how the *bodhisattva* fulfilled the *sīlapāramitā*. He fulfilled *sīla* not only as a human being but also as an animal. *Silavanāgarājajātaka, Sīlavīmaṃsajātaka, Devadhammajātaka, Lakkhanamigajātaka* and *Mahāsīlavajātak* are the examples.

In *Cakkavattisīhanādasutta* we can find the ten qualities of *cakkavatti* or universal monarch. There is also found *sīla* as an essential quality.[3] There are tenfold *kusalakammā*s (wholesome) in Buddhism. They are also called as *dasapuññakiriyavatthu*. There also one can find *sīla* as second limb.[4] Threefold *puññakiriyā*s are *dāna, sīla* and *bhāvanā*. *Sīla* is an essential category there too.

Buddhism does not judge one's quality or morality from one's external appearance. *Sīla* is not an external quality at all. Once Buddha mentions the monks, there are people those who are just like nice clay made earnings or gold plated iron coins. They are very attractive. They wonder big crowed. They are externally very attractive but internally seduced (*anto asuddhā bahi sobhamānā*).[5]

In *Soṇadaṇḍasutta of Dīghanikāya* Buddha had a discussion with Soṇadaṇḍa brāhmaṇa. There the Buddha explains that, just like hand washed by the hand, leg washed by the leg *sīla* is well purified by *paññā* and *paññā* is well purified by *sīla*.[6] There he has given the connection between the wisdom and morality.

"Or, *Kassapa,* there are ascetics who are talking about *sīla*. They are talking on *sīla* in various aspects. But I cannot

---

1. *Buddhavamsa Aṭṭhakathā, Dīpaṅkarabuddhavaṇṇanā,* (V.R.I.), p. 67.
2. *Buddhavaṃsapāli, Ratanacaṅkamaṇakhaṇḍa,* (V.R.I.), p. 34.
3. *DN., Pāṭhikavagga, Cakkavattisutta,* (V.R.I.), p. 44:
Pāṇā na hantabbo, adinnan nāditabbaṁ, kāmesumicchā na caritabbaṁ, musā na bhāsitabbaṁ majja na pātabbaṁ...
4. *Nāmarūpapariccheda, Pañcamo Paricchedo,* (V.R.I.), 42:
Dānaṁsīlaṁ bhāvanā ca, veyyāvaccapacāyanā ।
Pattānumodanā patti-dānan dhammassa desanā।
Savaṇan diṭṭhijukamma-miccevan dasadhā ṭhitaṁ।।
5. *S.N., Sagāthakavagga, Kosalasṃyutta, Sattajaṭilasutta,* (V.R.I.), p. 96.
6. *DN., Sīlakkhandhavagga, Soṇadaṇḍasutta,* (V.R.I.), p. 108.

find there anyone who is equivalent to me. That is nothing but *adhisīla* of what the Buddha possesses."[1]

According to this Buddha has mentioned whether there is *sīla,* that is something else what is practised by the ascetics. There are two *Sattajaṭila sūtra*s in *Saṁyuttanikāya* and *Udānapāli*. In the same way in *Taṇhāsutta* of *Mahāvaggapāli* the same thing occurs, "*sīla* should be known with association, not by short period, but the long period. In the same way it should be known by the wise people but not by the stupid".[2]

Noble Life of Upāsaka and Upāsikā in Buddhism (*Gahaṭṭhasīla*)

Buddhist householders are divided into two groups as *upāsaka*s and *upāsikā*s. There are the two assembles. Both these assemblies play a vital role in Buddhism. So they are called *sāvaka,* male assistants and *sāvikā* female assistants to the Buddha's dispensation. The role of *upāsaka* assembly is obvious. The role of *upāsikā* assembly also has an important place in Buddhism. It has its deep impact in the Buddhist history for propagating the Dhamma in India and abroad as a voluntary group of guides and donors (*dāyaka* and *dāyikā*).

A female householder as an *upāsikā* can enjoy a life with a good husband and children and can do household and social work by adhering to the Buddhist principles while following a pious life. Her first aim should be to maintain a good family life, looking after children, cattle, paddy fields, and maintaining household works well. If she wishes, of course, she can follow the path of renunciation practising moral principles (*sīla*), concentration (*samādhi*) and insight (*pañña*).[3]

There are five misdeeds which a person can refrain from doing hence negative actions as mentioned above, according to the *Dhammikasutta* can be classified further, into fifteenfold negative actions (misdeeds) as follows:

(i) The householder does not kill any living being.
The householder does not cause to kill any living being.

1. *DN., Sīlakkhandavagga, Mahāsīhanādasutta,* (V.R.I.), p. 155.
2. *SN., Kosalasaṃyutta, Sagātakavagga, Sattajaṭilasutta,* (V.R.I.), p. 96.
3. *SN., Devaputtasaṃyutta, Jatāsutta,* (V.R.I.), p. 16.

The householder does not approve of others' killing.

(ii) The householder abstains from taking anything that has not been given to him.
The householder abstains from causing anyone else to take what is not given to him.
The householder abstains from approving of it.

(iii) The householder abstains resorting to misconduct with a woman.
The householder abstains from causing other to do so.
The householder abstains from approving of it.

(iv) The householder does not speak a lie.
The householder does not cause others to speak falsely.
The householder does not approve of it.

(v) The householder does not take intoxicating drinks.
The householder does not cause others to take intoxicating drinks.
The householder does not approve others taking intoxicating drinks.

The above fifteen acts are described as institutions of negative actions *apuññāyatana.*[1] The misdeeds that are narrated in the *Āmagandhasutta* are as follows:[2] 1. Doing harmful acts on living beings, 2. Killing, 3. Cutting, 4. Binding, 5. Stealing, 6. Speaking falsehood, 7. Fraud, 8. Deception, 9. Worthless reading, 10. Intercourse with another's wife. A householder must not resort to bribing; he who does such a misdeed is called the lowest man (*narādhama*).

Further, a person who does not have compassion for living beings, who is cruel, is called immoral (*dussīla*). If a Buddhist householder does such immoral acts as mentioned above, he is not capable of being a good householder. Therefore, he is advised to avoid such acts.

The *Suttanipāta* furthermore points out several immoral acts in the *Parābhavasutta* and the *Vasalasutta* that should not be done by the householders. The Buddha had described such a person as a loser and an outcast and warns that one should not do such acts. He had also enumerated and given explanation of such misdeeds as

1. *St. N., Cūlavagga, Dhammikasutta,* (V.R.I.), pp. 139-42.
2. *St. N., Cūlavagga, Āmagandhasutta,* (V.R.I.), pp. 120-21.

follows: a person who is well off but does not treat his father and mother, is regarded as "a loser" and an "outcast". A person who does not give anything to a brāhmaṇa, samaṇa, friend or others and does not return those things that were taken by him and enjoys only by himself his wealth, is regarded as "a loser" and "outcast".

A married person who misbehaves with the other ladies or with the wives of relatives or friends is a loser and an outcast.

The *Parābhavasutta* gives a list of persons whose company should be given up by the householder. They are as follows:[1] He who hates the *dhamma,* 2. He who is with bad persons, 3. A sleepy, lazy and ill tempered person, 4. A person who goes after others' women, drinks alcohol and does gambling, 5. An old person jealous of her young wife, 6. A person who is uncontrolled in mind and lazy, is keeping supremacy, 7. A poor person who is born in "Khatthiya" caste but desires the crown of the country. The Buddhist householder must keep these persons far away.

Another list of persons who are regarded as outcasts (*vasala*) according to the *Vasalasutta* are as follows:[2]

1. A person who takes a debt and runs away;
2. A person who takes the life of other people;
3. A person who takes his relatives badly;
4. A person who praises himself and despises others;
5. A person who misleads his friends; and
6. A person who does misdeeds secretly.

In the *Maṅgalasutta,* the Buddha describes these persons as fools and advises not to associate them. A good householder should not associate these bad persons and should not follow their misdeeds because through these misdeeds there is degeneration and loss of his reputation in the society and will reborn in a woeful state after death.[3]

In this context one should also know that due to evil desires the following arise: 1. disputes, 2. tension, 3. lamentation, 4. sorrow, 5. envy, 6. arrogance, 7. conceit, and 8. slandering. Furthermore, he must believe in the Buddhist *kamma* theory and avoid the tenfold

---

1. *St. N., Uragavagga, Parābhavasutta,* (V.R.I.), pp. 100-102.
2. *St. N., Uragavagga, Vasasutta,* (V.R.I.), pp. 103-06.
3. *K.P., Maṅgalasutta,* (V.R.I.), pp. 4-5.

wrong views.[1]

Abstention from these evil deeds lends supports to the householder in gaining good reputation in the society. Then he becomes capable in following the five precepts (*pañcaśīla*), eight precepts (*aṭṭhaṅgasīla*), concentration (*samādhi*), and wisdom (*paññā*) also.

Buddhism is not merely a philosophy; it is also a guide to good behaviour. A person achieves the ultimate goal of Buddhism only through acting according to the Dhamma. Here the performance of good deeds is the path of committing wholesome acts (*kusalakamma*). Therefore, the concept of goods deeds (*paññākamma*) runs through the whole Buddhist doctrine as a connecting link.

Coming to this point it is necessary to say something about and main tenets or dogmas of Theravāda Buddhism. These are as follows:

(i) The four noble truth (*cattāri ariyasaccāni*)
(ii) The eightfold path (*ariyo aṭṭhaṅgiko maggo*)
(iii) Three characteristics of the world (*tilakhaṇa*)
(iv) Morality, Concentration and Wisdom (*ti sikkhā*)
(v) The theory of no soul (*anattavāda*)
(vi) Emancipation (*nibhāna*)
(vii) Action and rebirth (*kamma* and *patisandhi*)
(viii) Sublime way of life (*brahmavihāra*)
(ix) Theory of momentariness (*khaṇabhaṅguravāda*).

It is not possible here to elaborate all the above-mentioned theories due to paucity of space. But the author has just put these theories for the sake of comparison. *Sīla* can be connected to all these major teachings of Buddhism. For instance *dukkhanirodhagāminī paṭipadā ariyasacca* is divided into three steps. One step is *sīla*. Again the eightfold path is also divided into three parts. Among these parts *sīla* is the beginning limb. Thus, we come to conclusion *sīla* as an essential teachings for all the so-called theories in Budhism.

---

1. *DN*, *Sīlakkhandavaggapāli*, *Lohiccasutta*, (V.R.I.), p. 210.

3
Concept of Sīla in Jainism

Jainism like Buddhism also believes in reasoning. Therefore, one author says that—"it stresses the perfection of knowledge and teaches as its fundamental doctrine, the ethical evolution of man."[1] In Jainism mental purity is given emphasis not the external appearance. Rather mental purity is the source of constant tranquillity and emancipation.[2]

Origin, Antiquity and Spread of Jainism

According to popular Jaina beliefs twenty-four *tīrthaṅkara*s appear in every *kalpa*. Ṛṣabhadeva is said to be the first *tīrthaṅkara* of the present era. It is said that he taught seventy-two arts (*bāvottariṁ kalāo*) to men and sixty-four to women.[3]

Jainism is said to be started by Mahāvīra about whom something have been told in the preceding chapter. Here it can be said that even in the Vedic literature the term *vrātya*s are found. Perhaps the term *vrātya*s are used for Jain ascetics.[4]

It is also told that term *ṣabha* is used in the Ṛgvedic literature. Scholars say that it is perhaps about Ṛṣabhadeva the first *tīrthaṅkara* of Jainas that the Vedic literature mentions.

Spread of Jainism

Magadha seems to be the centre of attraction of various heretical

1. *Jainism in Buddhist Literature,* p. 21.
2. *Ibid.*
3. *Ibid.*, p. 22.
4. *Sanskrit-English Dictionary,* p. 741. I owe it to *Jainism in Buddhist Literature,* p. 22.

teachers. In the *Tripiṭaka* it is frequently found that the Buddha was preaching at Nālandā, Rājagaha and Vaiśālī, etc. It is said that the Buddha came across the Jaina ascetics at Kālasilā on the side of Isigili mountain in Rajagaba.[1] And he could not convince the Jaina ascetics regarding his views. Perhaps Jaina ascetics were following one of two extremes, i.e. self-mortification (*attakilmathānuyoga*) for nullifying the effect of past *karma*s and attaining emancipation. The Buddha's teachings did not go to deaf ears and he was able to convert Upāli Gahapati, Abhayarājakumāra and the lay devotee of Nigaṇṭha Nāthaputta, Asibandhakaputta Gāmini.[2]

Another area where Jainism go good ground was Kosala. Here also various follower of Nigaṇṭha Nāthaputta were in discussion with the Buddha. Two places in Kosala *janapada* were Śrāvastī and Sāketa where various Jaina followers were there. In Sāvatthī one rich banker (*seṭṭhī*) Migāra is said to be the follower of Jainism.

The other areas where Jainism spread during the time of the Buddha were Kapilavastu and Devadaha. Vappa Śākya, who was converted to Buddhism by Mogallāna earlier was a follower of Jainism. Vesāli was also a place where followers of Jainism were present. Examples of Saccaka, Sallaka and Sīha (a general of Licchavīs) can be taken who were followers of Jainism and later became the supporters of the Buddha. Here name of the Mallas of Pāvā can also be mentioned. Varanasi, Mithilā and Kauśāmbī, can be mentioned as places where Jainism was present at the time of the Buddha but the Pāli literature does not mention about it. Nigaṇṭha Nāthaputta travelled across Bihar, Bengal and Uttar Pradesh. He got much help in missionary activities from his maternal uncle Ceṭaka, the king of Vaiśāli and his sons-in-law Udayana, Dadhivāhana Śatānīka, Caṇḍapradyota, Nandivardhana and Bimbisāra.[3]

In the modern times a sizeable number of population of Jaina people is there in Rajasthan, Haryana, Bihar, Karnataka and Gujarat, etc. They are mostly business communities, traders and stock-holders.

---

1. *Jainism in Buddhist Literature,* p. 43.
2. *Ibid.*, p. 44.
3. *Ibid.*, p. 46.

Philosophical Literature of Jainism

Jainism has contributed a lot in the development of philosophical literature of India. Every religion has a great mass of literature. But all literature does not provide philosophical aspect. Philosophy is one thing and preaching is another. Philosophical teachings provide food for intellectual brain. Therefore, it seems necessary here to provide content of philosophical literature of Jainism. These philosophical literature can be divided into four schools.[1]

(a) Canonical School (up to sixth century)
(b) Anekānta School (from third century A.D. to eighth century A.D.)
(c) Pramāṇa School (from eighth century A.D. to seventeenth century A.D.)
(d) Navya-Nyāya School (from seventeenth century A.D.).

Canonical School

The Canonical Literature of Jainas draws its source from the Mahāvīra or Nigaṇṭha Nāthaputta. It is said that the disciple of Mahāvīra named Indrabhūti or Gautama collected the canonical literature from his Master Mahāvīra. He (Indrabhūti) died at the age of ninety-two at Rājagaha.[2]

Digambara tradition emphasizes that after death of Indrabhūti for many years rather a long period of time successors of the Master could not gain proficiency in all the *aṅga*s. But the Śvetāmbara tradition is of the opinion that this tradition preserved the *aṅga*s and *upāṅga*s. Here it is important to mention that Jainism and its various *ācāryā*s preserved the literature through *śruti paramparā* (recitation tradition). In this tradition a teacher hands down its knowledge to his disciples. In course of time the disciples become the teachers and in this way the tradition is continued. Some scholars believe that for the sake of supremacy, the Śvetāmbara tradition added some more materials in the *aṅga*s and *upāṅga*s. These are described hereunder.

---

1. M.K. Jain, *Jain Darśana*, p. 14. But here I owe it to *Jainism in Buddhist Literature,* p. 33.
2. *Jainism in Buddhist Literature,* p. 34.

The Twelve Aṅgas

(i) *Āyāraṅga*,
(ii) *Sūyagaḍaṅga*,
(iii) *Thāṇāṅga*,
(iv) *Samavāyāṅga*,
(v) *Viyāhapaṇṇatti* or Bhagavatī,
(vi) *Nāyādhammakahāo*,
(vii) *Uvāsagadasāo*,
(viii) *Antagaḍadasāo*,
(ix) *Aṇuttarovaiyadasāo*,
(x) *Paṇhāvāgaraṇāiṃ*,
(xi) *Vivagasuya*,
(xii) *Diṭṭhivāya*.

The Twelve Upāṅgas

(i) *Ovavāiya*,
(ii) *Rāyapaseṇaijja*,
(iii) *Jivābhigama*,
(iv) *Pannavaṇā*,
(v) *Suriyapaṇṇatti*,
(vi) *Jambuddivapaṇṇatti*,
(vii) *Canapaṇṇatti*,
(viii) *Niryāvalio*,
(ix) *Kappāvaḍamsiāo*,
(x) *Pupphiāo*,
(xi) *Pupphacūliāo*,
(xii) *Vaṇhidāsāo*.

The Ten Paiṇṇas

(i) *Causaraṇa*,
(ii) *Āurapaccakkhāṇa*,
(iii) *Bhattapariṇṇaya*,
(iv) *Saṃthāraga*,
(v) *Taṇḍulaveyāliya*
(vi) *Candāvijjhaya*,[1]

---

1. *Prāk ta Sāhitya Kā Itihāsa* by Dr. Jagadisachandra Jain, pp. 48-50—The name of these two books are not in the list of this book. In place of these two books we find *Gaccāyāra* and *Maraṇasamāhī*.

(vii) *Devindatthaya,*
(viii) *Gaṇivijjā,*
(ix) *Mahāpaccakkāṇa,*
(x) *Viratthava.*

The Six Cheyasuttas

(i) *Nisīha,*
(ii) *Mahānisīha,*
(iii) *Vavahāra,*
(iv) *Āyārādasāo* or *Dasāsuyakkandha,*
(v) *Kappa* (*B hatkalpa*),
(vi) *Pañcakappa* or *Jīyakalpa.*

The Four Mūlasuttas

(i) *Uttarājjhaya* (*Uttarājjhayaṇ*)
(ii) *Dasaveyāliya*
(iii) *Āvassaya*
(iv) *Piṇḍamijjutti.*[1]

The Two Cūḷikā Suttas

(i) *Nandī*
(ii) *Anuyogadāra.*[2]

In Magadha the *ācārya*s had to flee south under the leadership of Visākācārya. When this teacher returned to Magadha he found that pupils of Sthūlabhadra (who stayed in Magadha and did not go to the south) had nourished attachment to clothes. Digambara have also preserved their literature. These literatures seems to be the same but there are some changes too. The Digambara canonical literature is divided into two parts.[3] These are *Aṅgapraviṣṭa* and *Aṅgabāhya.*

1. In the above-mentioned book the other name of this text has been given as *Ohanijjutti,* p. 50.
2. *Jainism in Buddhist Literature,* pp. 34-35.
3. *Ibid.*, p. 38.

Aṅgapraviṣṭa

This *Aṅgrapraviṣṭa* of Digambara canon is the same as the canon of Śvetāmbara. There is a little difference. The last *aṅga* of the Śvetāmbara is *Diṭṭhivaya* or *D ṣṭipravāda.* It is of five kinds. These are –

(i) Five *parikarma*
(ii) *Sūtra*
(iii) Four *Anuyoga*
(iv) *Pūrvagatas*
(v) Five *cūlikā*s.

The first is five *parikarmā*s. It is further divided into following books:[1]

(i) *Candaprajñapti*
(ii) *Sūryaprajñapti*
(iii) *Jambudvīpaprajñapti*
(iv) *Dvīpaprajñapti*
(v) *Vyākhyāprajñapti.*

There is no division of *sūtra*s, whereas *Anuyogas* are as follows:[2]

(i) *Prathamānuyoga*
(ii) *Karaṇānuyoga*
(iii) *Dravyānuyoga*
(iv) *Caraṇānuyoga.*

In addition to this as there are 15 texts under the *Khuddaka Nikāya* so there are texts under the *pūrvagata*s. These are as follows:

(i) *Utpādapūrva*
(ii) *Agrāyaṇī*
(iii) *Vīryānuvāda*

---

1. *Jainism in Buddhist Literature,* p. 38.
2. Ibid.

(iv) *Astināstipravāda*
(v) *Jñānapravāda*
(vi) *Saṭpravāda*
(vii) *Ātmapravāda*
(viii) *Karamapravāda*
(ix) *Pratyākhyāna*
(x) *Vidyānuvāda*
(xi) *Kalyāṇavāda*
(xii) *Prāṇavāda*
(xiii) *Kriyāvāda*
(xiv) *Trilokavindusāra.*

Note only this the last one, i.e. five *cūlikā*s are as follows:[1]

(a) *Jalagata*
(b) *Sthalagata*
(c) *Māyāgata*
(d) *Rūpagata*
(e) *Ākāśagata*

Aṅgabāyha Sutta

This is the second main division of the Digambara literature. It is divided into fourteen *prakīrṇaka*s.[2] These are as follows:

(i) *Sāmāyika*
(ii) *Saṃstava*
(iii) *Vandanā*
(iv) *Pratikramaṇa*
(v) *Vinayana*
(vi) *K tikarma*
(vii) *Dasavaikālika*
(viii) *Uttarādhyayana*
(ix) *Kalpavyavahāra*
(x) *Kalpākalpa*
(xi) *Mahākalpa Saṁjñaka*
(xii) *Puṇḍarīka*

1. *Jainism in Buddhist Literature,* p. 38.
2. *Ibid.*

(xiii) *Mahāpuṇḍarīka*
(xiv) *Nisiddhika.*

Anekānta School

In every religion there are some important books, which play vital role in shaping various philosophies. For example, in Buddhism, the *Milindapañha*[1] is such a book which provides very important philosophical aspect of Buddhism. It is full with similes and examples by which major and abstruse philosophies of Buddhism are explained. In the same way one can see the Anekānta school for Jainism.

Puṣpadanta and Bhūtāvalī wrote a joint work named *Satkhaṇḍāgama.*[2] As both of them wrote the above-mentioned book, so Puṣpadanta wrote the beginning portion and Bhūtāvalī the latter part. The another important book was written by Gauṇadharācārya named as *Kaṣāyapāhuḍa.* This book was written on the basis of *Pejjadosaprābh ta* of Jñānapravādaputva during the first century B.C.E.[3] There are such works as provide foundation to later Jaina philosophies particularly for Digambara sect.

These works contain rudiments of Jaina philosophies. On these works later *ācārya*s like Kundakunda, Umāsvātī and Samantabhadra wrote. As already stated there was a great famine in Magadha. Due to that famine Digambaras thought that their literature was lost. Therefore, in absence of original canon, the Digambaras recognizes works of Puṣpadanta, Bhūtāvalī, Guṇadharācārya, Kundakunda, Svāmī Kārttikeya, Umāsvātī, Vaṭṭakera and Śivārya as canonical works.[4] Here it is also important to mention that period of Anekānta school is marked by the establishment of the Syādvāda conception with greater emphasis. The *Saptabhaṅgī* of Ācārya Kundakunda is developed by Samantabhadra, Siddhasena, Sumati, Pātrekasarī and Śrīdatta. A complete discussion of all the doctrines of Jainism is the characteristics of this age.[5]

---

1. *Milindapañha,* V.R.I. edition.
2. *Jainism in Buddhist Literature,* pp. 39-40.
3. *Ibid.,* p. 40.
4. *Ibid.*
5. *Ibid.,* p. 41.

Pramāṇa School

During this period a revolutionary theory was evolved. This theory was concept of *pratyakṣa*. It is denoted in English as indicated knowledge.[1] Before this period Āgamic tradition accepted *pratyakṣa* as direct cognition. The belief of indicated knowledge has its own basis. It is said that there would be no direct cognition when sense organs rely upon empirical experience. Realization through mental perception is called as transcendental perception. It is said that Jinabhadra Kṣmāśramaṇa divided the *pramāṇas* systematically into two types. These are *saṃvyāvahārika pratyakṣa* (transcendental perception).

This period saw in the rise of Buddhist logicians. Special mention can be made of *Pramāṇavārtika* of Dhammakīrti. Devendramati wrote commentary on it which is known as *Pramāṇavārtikaṭīkā*. Another book of the genre of logic was *Pramāṇavārtikālaṅkāra* of Prajñākaragupta. *Tattvasaṃgraha* of Śāntarakṣita was also an important book of logic. All these logicians and their works refuted Vedic views and Jaina views of Umāsvāmī, Samantabhadra and Siddhasena. At this critical moment, writes one author, "Acarya Akalanka and Haribhadra entered the field of controversy against the opponents of Jainism."[2]

Ācārya Akalaṅka was very prominent in that age. He wrote *Tattvārthavārtikā, Astasati, Waghiyastrayasrav tti, Nyāyaviniścaya, Saviv tti, Siddhiviniścaya* and *Pramāṇasaṃgraha*, etc.[3] All these writings categorically denied the thoughts of Dharmakīrti and others. It is said to be very effective from the Jaina point of view. His satirical and effective arguments supported Jainism in a nice way.

In the same way Haribhadra and his works supported a lot to Jaina followers. His works like *Śāstravārtāsamuccaya, Anekāntajayapatākā* and *Anekāntavādapraveśa* supported the view-points of Jainism and its followers. Jaina followers got in the form of Akalaṅka and Haribhadra as epitome personalities and they again rallied after Jainism.

Deliverance of soul according to Jainism is only possible

---

1. *Jainism in Buddhist Literature.*
2. *Ibid.*, p. 42.
3. *Ibid.*

through ethical discipline.[1] Emancipation of soul from repeated births is possible only by strict discipline. This discipline is essential for attaining goal. The aim or goal in Jaina religion is attainment of complete conquest of attachment and realization.[2] This discipline is narrated in Jainism by some scholars as householders conduct.[3] Some scholar describes it as duties of householders.[4] Whatever it be it is important have to say that the whole life of Jaina monks or householder is full of moral codes. The same is applicable in the case of Buddhist monks and lay devotees too. But the aim of the author is to deal with morality which is essential for Jaina monks and householders to become free from kārmic actions and to attain liberation.

Like *dasasīla* of Buddhism, Jainism has *pañcapāpa* (five faults).[5] These are as follows:

(i) *Hiṃsā* (injury)
(ii) *Asatya* (falsehood)
(iii) *Steya* (stealing)
(iv) *Abrahmacarya* (unchastity)
(v) *Parigraha* (worldly attachment).

These vows are generally divided into two parts, e.g. *aṇuvrata*s (partial vows). It can also be denoted as limited abstention from the five aforesaid evils and *mahāvrata*s (total abstention from five faults).[6] In Theravāda Buddhism *dasasīla* or *dasa sikkhāpada* is meant for both lay followers (*upāsaka* and *upāsikā*) and monks (*bhikkhu*). The first five or first eight are for lay people. It is in this way that a lay followers when wants to become pious has to observe first five precepts. When he moves further on the path he observes three more precepts. Therefore, first five or first eight are valid for lay people. Ten precepts are exclusively for monks and nuns. In the same way *aṇuvrata*s are for householders and the *mahāvrata*s for *śramaṇa*s.

---

1. *Jainism in Buddhist Literature*, p. 93.
2. Jinendra Varni, *Samaṇ Suttam,* Introduction, p. XV.
3. *Ibid*., p. XIX.
4. Bhagacandra Jain, *Jainism in Buddhist Literature,* p. 92.
5. *Ibid*., p. 93.
6. *Ibid*.

The famous ācārya Kundakunda Swāmī narrated householders duties on the basis of *pratimās*. He advocated three *guṇavrata*s and four *śikṣāvrata*s.[1] These are as follows:

***Three Guṇavratās*[2]**

(i) *Dikparimāṇa*
(ii) *Anarthadaṇḍavarjana*
(iii) *Bhogopabhogaparimāṇa.*

Four Śikṣāvratas

(i) *Sāmāyika*
(ii) *Prosadha*
(iii) *Atithipūjā*
(iv) *Sallekhanā.*

Some *ācāryā*s made a little change in the above list. As for example Swāmī Kārttīkeya replaced *sallekhanā* with *deśavākāsika*. For do find another *ācārya* who again included *sallekhanā* in *śikṣāvrata*s.[3] In the *Tattvārtthasutta* the morality (*sīla*) is not divided into *guṇavrata*s and *śiksāvrata*s but only seven kinds of morality are prescribed. These are as follows:

(i) *Digvirati*
(ii) *Deśavirati*
(iii) *Anarthadaṇḍa*
(iv) *Sāmāyika*
(v) *Prosadhopavāsa*
(vi) *Bhogopabhogaparimāṇa*
(vii) *Atithisaṃvibhāga.*

In this calculation *salekhanā* was described separately.

There are some scholars who describe householders' duties on the basis of twelve *vratas*.[4] These twelve *vrata*s are five *aṇuvrata*s

---

1. Ācārya Kunthusāgara, *Śrāvakadharmapradīpa,* p. 5.
2. *Jainism in Buddhist Literature,* p. 93.
3. *Śrāvakadharmapradīpa,* p. 5.
4. *Jaiism in Buddhist Literature,* p. 93.

(small vows or limited abstention), three *guṇavrata*s (strengthening vows) and four *śiksāvrata*s (disciplinary vows). These can be enumerated as follows:

(a) Five *aṇuvrata*s
   (i) *ahiṃsā* (injury)
   (ii) *asatya* (falsehood)
   (iii) *steya* (stealing)
   (iv) *abrahmacarya* (unchastity)
   (v) *parigraha* (worldly attachment).
(b) Three *guṇavrata*s (strengthening vows)
   (i) *digvrata*
   (ii) *deśavrata*
   (iii) *anarthadaṇḍavrata.*
(c) Four *śikṣāvrata*s
   (i) *sāmāyika*
   (ii) *prosodhopavāsa*
   (iii) *upabhogaparibhogaparimāṇa*
   (iv) *atithisaṃvibhāga.*

Here the Ācārya Umāswāmī divided *vratī* (followers of *rata*) into two categories.[1]

(i) *agārī*—who follow *aṇuvrata*s
(ii) *anāgārī*—who follows *mahāvrata*s.

Notably, Ācārya Umāswāmī took pains and described the *aticāra*s of each *vrata.*[2] But he did not mention *aṣṭa-mūlaguṇa*s and *pratimā*s. Ācārya Jinasena described the householders duties on the basis of *pakṣa* (beginner's course with favourable inclination towards the sacred law), *caryā* (performance of eleven *pratimā*s and *sādhanā* (the accomplishment of *sallekhanā*).[3]

Coming to this point it is necessary to say something about the source from where duties of householders in Jainism are drawn. Some of the sources have been mentioned. It is presented here in

---

1. *Jainism in Buddhist Literature,* p. 93.
2. *Ibid.*
3. *Ibid.*

brief together with writers and their books.[1]

Digambaras

Book	Author
a. *Cāritraprābh ta*	Kundakunda
b. *Tattvārthasūtra*	Umāsvāmī
c. *Ratnakaraṇḍaka*	Samantabhadra
d. *Upāsakādhyayana*	Somadeva
e. *Puruṣārthasiddhyupāya*	Am tacandra
f. *Śrāvakācāra*	Amitagati
g. *Śrāvakācāra*	Vasunandi
h. *Sāgara Dharmām ta*	Āsādhara
i. *Ādipurāṇa*	Jinasena
j. *Cāritrasāra*	Cāmuṇḍarāya
k. *Sāvaya-dhamma-dohā*	Anonymous
l. *Traivarṇikācāra*	Somasena

Śvetāmbara

Book	Author
a. *Sāvaya-paṇṇatti*	Umāsvātī
b. *Dharma-bindu*	Haribhadra
c. *Uvāsagadasāo*	Abhayadeva
d. *Yoga Śāstra*	Hemacandra
e. *Śrāddha-dina-k tya*	Devendra
f. *Ācāra-dinakara*	Vardhamāna
g. *Śrāddha-vidhi*	Ratnaśekhara

The above-mentioned books and their authors have been presented here on the basis of the book of R. Williams namely the

1. *Śrāvakācāra,* Jain code of conduct for householdres, p. 18.

Jain Yoga.[1] In preparing of the list of the books of householders the noted author has excluded the works of Tamil and Kannada treatises.[2] A great deal of Hindi and Gujarati books have also been excluded here.

One also should understand here that Right belief (*samyak-d ṣṭi samyaktva*), right conduct (*samyak-cāritra*) combined together lead to liberation or emancipation.[3] Right belief can be explained in several ways. But it is expressed in one way as perfect faith in the six-substances (*dravya*s) and in seven principles (*tattva*s). These two are said as the main dogmas of Jain religion.[4] Right knowledge can be explained as the knowledge of the principles of *tattva*s and *dravya*s. The third one—Right conduct (*samyak-cāritra*) is the accomplishment of ethical discipline or code of conduct. These codes of conduct are of two types:

(i) Code of conduct for monks and nuns (*yatyācāra*)
(ii) Code of conduct for laymen or householders (*śrāvakācāra*).

Here a discussion about the term *śrāvaka* is needed. It is a widely used term for lay people in Jainism. Coming to a question can be asked that who is *śrāvaka*?, the answer is "one who sincerely and regularly listens to the teachings and preaching of the Jina through the monk for the good of one's own self is a *śrāvaka*."[5] Other alternate term for the *śrāvaka* are *śramaṇopāsaka*, *sāgāra*, *g hin*, *g hastha* (one who practices the prescribed code of conduct by staying at home), *desa samyamin* (one who is practically self-restrained and is indifferent to worldly attachments), *śrāddha* (one having faith in the words of the Jina as taught by the monks), etc.[6] When Jainism was in a full-flow or widely famous then a layman was known as *śrāvaka*. Generally a term slowly gets corrupt among common masses and gets a different name. In the same way the term *śrāvaka* became corrupt and became *sarāvaga* or *sarāvagī*. During these days a person who respected Jina was simply known

1. R. Williams, *Jain yoga,* but here I owe it to *Śrāvakācāra,* pp. 17-18.
2. *Ibid.*, p. 18.
3. *Ibid.*, p. 17.
4. *Ibid.*, p. 10.
5. *Abhidhāna Rājendra,* here I owe it to *Śrāvakācāra,* p. 11.
6. *Ibid.*

as Jaina.

At this point description of *samyaktva* and *aṣṭamūlaguṇa*s is presented and later *vrata*s would be explained.

Samyaktva or Right belief (*samyak d ṣṭi*) is an important part of any work connected with lay people or with their duties. The other two parts of the three jewels, i.e. Right knowledge and Right conduct are based on the Right belief. According to *Uttarādhyayanasūtra* Right knowledge cannot be attained in absence of Right belief, acquirement of Right belief is impossible without Right knowledge, and without Right Conduct there can be no liberation.[1] According to Cāmuṇḍarāya, Amitagati and Vasunandi, etc., characteristics (*guṇa*) of *samyaktva*[2] are as follows:

(a) *saṃvega* – spiritual craving
(b) *sama, upasama* – tranquillity
(c) *nirveda* – disgust
(d) *bhakti* – devotion
(e) *anukampā* – compassion
(f) *nindā* – remorse
(g) *garhā* – repentance
(h) *vātsalya* – loving kindness.

In addition to this some *ācārya*s like Samantabhadra, Somadeva and Am tacandra, etc., have narrated following *aṅga*s (organs) of *samyaktva* in their works.[3]

(i) *niḥṣaṅka* – freedom from fear
(ii) *niḥkāṅkṣā* – desirelessness
(iii) *nirvicikitsā* – overcoming of repugnance
(iv) *amūḍha-d ṣṭi* – unswearing orthodoxy
(v) *prabhāvanā* – good works
(vi) *upagūhana* – edification
(vii) *sthiti-karaṇa* – strengthening the faith
(viii) *vātsalya* – loving kindness.

1. *Śrāvakācāra,* p. 26.
2. *Ibid.*, p. 27.
3. *Ibid.,* pp. 27-28.

Besides these, there are various kinds of *doṣa*s (blemishes), *aticāra*s (infractions) and *liṅga*s (characteristics) of *samayktva* mentioned in different texts.[1] For some *ācārya*s like Samantabhadra and Vasunandi Right Belief is described as faith in *āpta* (the Jina), *āgama* (the scriptures), *tattva*s and *padārthas*.[2] In the opinion of Hemacandra, right belief is faith in the Right *deva,* the Right *guru* and the right *dhamma*.[3]

The Mūla Guṇas

As already stated, every *ācārya* has not mentioned the *mūla guṇa*s. Here mention may be made of *ācārya* like Kundakunda and Umāswāmī. Contrary to this some *ācārya*s like Somadeva, Devasena and Padmanandi have presented the following *aṣṭa-mūla guṇa*s.[4]

(1-5) Abstention from five milky fruits like fig, etc.
(6) *māṃsa-virati* – abstention from meat
(7) *madya-virati* – abstention from wine
(8) *madhu-virati* – abstention from honey.

Some *ācārya*s mention all these *aṣṭa-mūla guṇa*s but do not all these with the same name. Ācārya Amitagati adds a new element named *arātribhojana* (refraining from taking food at night) in the above list of eight.[5] Here a discussion of *vrata*s seems necessary. Before explanation of *vratas,* a short explanation of *aticāra*s is given here.

The aticāra

While a householder pursues a vow, he must know about its *aticāra*. The meaning of the term *aticāra* is offences, infraction and transgressions, etc. It is attached to each vow. According to Ācārya Am tacandra *aticāra* is that which hampers the purity of the vow.[6]

1. *Śrāvakācāra,* pp. 27-32.
2. Vasunandi, *Śrāvakācāra,* p. 4, here I owe it to *Śrāvakācāra,* pp. 25-26.
3. *Yogaśāstra*, v.2. But here it has taken from *Śrāvakācāra,* p. 26.
4. *Śrāvakācāra,* pp. 35-36.
5. *Ibid.,* p. 36.
6. *Sagaradharmām ta,* VI-24.

Generally a monk advises a householder how to become cautions about the *aticāra*. And not to do offence. For example, for observing the vow of *ahiṃsā* householder is cautioned against the injury to living beings in respect of the following:[1]

(a) *bandha* – keeping captivity
(b) *vadha* – beating
(c) *chavicheda* – mutilating
(d) *atibhārāropaṇa* – overloading
(e) *bhaktapāna vyavaccheda* – depriving of food and drink.

The another term which is used in the sense of offence is *bhaṅga*. But both the terms, i.e. *bhaṅga* and *aticāra* have different connotation and different aspects too. A Śvetāmbara teacher makes distinction between *bhaṅga* and *aticāra* whereas the Digambara teachers do not do so.[2] In the case of *bhaṅga* a vow is totally negated while in a transgression, i.e. in *aticāra* a vow is partly completed and partly infringed.[3] In the text for example it is said that if a householder refuses to give alms is a *bhaṅga* of *dāna vrata*. But giving alms without respect is its *aticāra*.[4] Now a comment of each *vrata* is necessary. Starting is made with *anuvrata*s.

The Ahiṃsāṇuvrata (Vow of Non-killing)

Most of the Jaina literature agree with *ahiṃsāṇuvrata* and also recognize that it is the first of the five small or limited vows. The word *ahiṃsā* plays an important role in Jaina ethics or religion. It also holds the key position in the ethical discipline of the householder.

About *ahiṃsā* it is said that it is a maxim like word that has left an important mark on the minds of sages and householders. It is said that *jīvānaṁ rakkhaṇam dhammo*[5]–which means giving protection to living is (true) religion. About the true religion it is said that, so *dhammo jattha dayā,* i.e. the religion bases on compassion is the true religion.[6] If the religion is a tree then compassion root.

---

1. *Śrāvakācāra,* p. 48.
2. *Ibid.*
3. *Ibid.*
4. *Ibid.*, p. 49.
5. *Kārtikeyānuprekṣā,* V. 478, here I owe it to *Śrāvakācāra,* p. 50.
6. *Śrāvakācāra,* p. 50.

Therefore, it is said that *dayā mūla dhammaṅgivaha*[1]. Finding its great importance the Ācārya Am tacandra has tried to elucidate it and says that other *vrata* are other from of the first *vrata*, i.e. *ahiṃsāṇuvrata* and have been restarted in different terms.[2] The nature of this *vrata* has been elaborated by Svāmī Samantabhadra in a single verse in his book named the *Ratnakaraṇḍaka*. Its translation is given here:

> "Abstaining from intentionally injuring mobile living beings, through mind, words or body in any of three ways—directly, through somebody or by consent (i.e. in nine ways) is called *sthūla–vadhaviramaṇa* or *ahiṃsāṇu vrata* by the wise."[3]

The word *ahiṃsā* is the opposite word of *hiṃsā*. Here it is necessary to say something about *hiṃsā* from the point of view of Jainism. According to Umāsvāmī *hiṃsā* is severance of any of the vitalities (*prāṇas*) by one moved by passion.[4] In Jainism immobile beings (*sthāvara-jīvas*) possess for vitalities, e.g. touch, energy, respiration and span of life. These are known as *ekendriyas*. The mobile beings are in the possession of senses. These senses can be taste, smell, sight, hearing and speech. Therefore, it can be said that one who inflicts injury to living beings with passion or carelessness (*pramāda*), is guilty of *hiṃsā*.

Again this *hiṃsā* can be said of two forms, e.g. *sūkṣma-hiṃsā* and *sthūla-hiṃsā*. Destroying the life of an living being is *sūkṣma-hiṃsā*. When the life of a living being that has two senses or more is destroyed it is known as *sthūla-hiṃsā*. This *hiṃsā* may be inherent in one's occupation. In this case it is known as *ārambhaja-hiṃsā*. When it is not related to one's occupation it is called *anārambhaja-hiṃsā*. In another words, it is also called as *saṅkalpaja* or intentional injury.

Ācārya Am tacandra takes a critical view of this vow and says that one should not entertain the stupid idea that religion (religious merit) flourishes through good and hence, everything may be

1. *Ibid.*
2. *Ibid.*, p. 51.
3. *Ibid.*
4. *Ibid.*

offered to them and embodied beings (and offer them to gods).[1] Jainism is very critical about *hiṃsā* while dealing with other religion or creed. It is against the sacrifices of animals as depicted in Hinduism, Islam and Christianity, etc. In Hinduism there is one sect, i.e. *vaisṇava* which is against the violence or any kind of use of flesh. Thus it is said that in Jainism not only one abstains itself from all cruelties, but also preaches *āhiṃsā* as its first and foremost tenet.[2] It considers thought as the root of action.[3] Based on thought and action this *hiṃsā* is said to be of two kinds, e.g. *bhāva hiṃsā* and *dravya hiṃsā*. *Bhāva hiṃsā* refers to the injury aimed at level of thought, while *dravya hiṃsā* is the thought translated into action.[4]

Referring to this *vrata* it is said that a householder takes a vow not to kill or harm anyone or a living being. But if he is attacked or is in the verge of loosing property, nation, institutions and family, etc., then he can use force up to limited extent. Therefore, it is said that his agricultural, industrial, occupational and diverse living activities do also involves injury to life, but it should be limited to the minimum possible, through carefulness, clarity and due precaution.[5] In Jainism a householder is advised to refrain from intentional injury and not the other kind of injury which is unavoidable and in one sense or the other is necessary.[6] Am tacandra discusses three kinds of *hiṃsā,* e.g. *k ta* (done by self), *kārita* (got done by agents) and *anumata* (approved).[7] It is already narrated that there are five kinds of *aticāra* (transgression) of this vow of *ahiṃsā*. There are *bandha, vadha, chaviccheda, atibhāra* and *annapānanirodha*.

Ahiṃsā is the basic principle of almost every major religion of the world. The Buddha is said to be the compassionate incarnation of Viṣṇu in India. The Allah of Muslims is called merciful (*al-raheem*) and beneficent (*al-rahmān*).[8] In Hindustan the god is said as *dayālu* (compassionate). In Bible it is also a part of

1. *Upāsakādhyayana* V. 331; here the author has taken from *Śrāvakācāra,* p. 59.
2. *Householders Discipline in Jainism,* p. 29.
3. *Ibid*., pp. 29-30.
4. *Ibid*., p. 30.
5. *Religion and Culture in Jainism,* p. 30.
6. *Ibid*., p. 30.
7. *Householders Discipline in Jainism,* p. 32.
8. *Householdere's Discipline in Jainism,* pp. 28-29.

commandment. In *Mahābhārata* it is said that the eighteen Purāṇas have been condensed by Vyāsa in two phrases: The good of others lead to religious merit, causing pain to others is seen.[1]

There are a number of stories also related to this *ahiṃsāṇuvrata*. One story comes in the *Uttarādhyayana*. Ariṣṭanemi was a cousin of Śrī K ṣṇa. One day he went in the armoury and blew the conch of Śrī K ṣṇa, called *pāñcajanya*. The whole city of Dvārikā quivered as if an earthquake had occurred. Śri K ṣṇa, came to the armoury and found Ariṣṭanemi blowing the conch. There were all pleasantly surprised to discover his wonderful prowess. They made a proposal for celebrating his marriage. After a great deal of persuasion, Ariṣṭanemi accepted the proposal. The marriage was settled with a princess of Mathurā. The bridal party went there in great pomp. Ariṣṭanemi heard the piteous shrieking of birds and beasts. He made an inquiry and came to know that the all those unfortunate creatures were kept in pan to provide food for the marriage party. He was stricken with mercy for the helpless mute animals and declined to marry.[2]

The Satyāṇuvrata (Vow of Truthfulness)

This is the second vow of the five partial vows. It refers to the total abstinence from untruth and adherence of truth at the same time.[3] For some religion it may be metaphysical entity, but in Jainism it is explained as ethical principle.[4] It is important to note here that in Buddhism it comes under *musāvāda veramaṇī* of the Ten Precepts (*dasasikkhāpada*). The great Ācārya Am tacandra defines the opposite of *satya* and explains what the non-truth is.[5]

"Whatever any wrong statement is made through

1. *Ibid.*
2. *Uttarājjhayāna,* xxii, I owe this reference to, Acharya Tulsi, *Illumination of Jaina Tenets,* p. 165.
3. *Illumination of Jaina Tenets,* p. 38.
4. *Ibid.*
5. *Illumination of Jaina Tenets*, p. 38, in fact it is the translation of the *Puruṣārthasiddhyupāya*, V. 91, p. 81.
Yaddidaṁ pramādayogā dasadabhidhānaṁ vidhīyate kimapi |
Tadan tamapi vijñeyaṁ tadbhedaḥ santi catvāraḥ ||

pramādayoga (careless activity of body, mind and speech), it is certainly known as falsehood."

The above-mentioned *pramāda-yoga* has been explained in following four ways.[1]

(i) Denying the existence of a thing with its position, time and nature while that object actually exists. For example, it is said that "Devadatta is not here" when he is actually present there.
(ii) Assertion made for a thing regarding position, time and place when it does not exist at all. As for example, "the pitcher is here" when it is not there.
(iii) Presentation of a thing as something different from what it really is. As for example—a horse is said to be a cow.
(iv) It is about a speech or talk which is despicable, condemnable or sinful or disagreeable.

Ācārya Samantabhadra explains it in the following way.[2]

> "abstaining from speaking oneself and from making others to speak gross falsehood and also from truth that causes injury to others is called *satyāṇuvrata,* the minor vow of truthfulness by the saints."

There are five *aticāra*s of this vow. These *aticāra*s have been explained by Am tacandra as follows:[3]

1. *mithyopadesadāna* — false preaching and advice.
2. *rahasobhyākhyāna* — divulging one's secret.
3. *kūṭalekhak ti* — forgery
4. *nyāsapahāra* — breach of trust.
5. *sākāramantrabheda* — disclosing inferences drawn from gesture.

In *Ṛgveda* truth is represented by the term ta. *Śatapatha*

1. *Śrāvakācāra,* p. 64.
2. *Ibid.,* p. 63.
3. *Ibid.,* pp. 40-41.

Brāhmaṇa equates truth with *dharma*. In the *Upaniṣad,* truth is called ultimate reality.[1]

In Buddhism truth is divided into two parts, e.g. *paramattha sacca* (Ultimate truth) and *sammuti sacca* (Conventional truth).[2]

Acauryāṇuvrata (Vow of Non-stealing)

This is the third among the five partial vows. It signifies abstention from accepting a thing which is not given.[3] This vow is also equated with another term as – *adattādānagrahana*.[4] It is also explained as – "careless taking of anything which is not given is deemed as theft, and that is *hiṃsā*".[5] According to Umāsvāmī, "stealing as taking anything which is not given; and this amounts to theft if the activity is actuated by passion".[6] Another great Ācārya Samantabhadra describes it's appose in detail. According to him—"he who does not appropriate to himself, not give away to any one else, the property of another, which is placed, dropped, forgotten or deposited by him, is said to observe the householder's vow of non-stealing".

Like previous vows, this *vrata* has also its transgression given by *ācāryas*. According to Am tacandra followings are the five *aticāras* of this vow.[7]

(i) *pratirpavyavahāraḥ*—adulteration
(ii) *stenaniyogaḥ*—instigating theft
(iii) *tadh tadānaṁ*—receiving stolen property
(iv) *rājavirodhātikarama*—violating state rules
(v) *hīnādhikamānakaraṇa*—false weight and measures.

From a glimpse at above transgressions, it can be said that from

1. *A Manual of Abhidhamma,* p. 6.
2. *Householder's Discipline in Jainism,* p. 41.
3. *Ibid.*
4. *Ibid.*
5. *Śrāvakācāra,* p. 66.
6. *Ibid.*
7. *Householder's Discipline in Jainism,* p. 42. Also in the verse no. 185 of the same book on p. 89:
Pratirūpakavyavahāraḥ-stenariyogastadāha tadānam |
Rājavirodhaghātikaramahīnādhikamānakaraṇe ca ||

the very beginning efforts were taken to preserve the state. In preserving state certainly one kind or the other *hiṃsā* involved in that process. Therefore, Jainism gave much prominence on *hiṃsā* which is not seen in Buddhism. That is why Jainas gave attention trade particularly of finished goods.

Brahmacariyāṇuvrata (Vow of Celibacy)

Ācārya Am tacandra advises householders to renounce non-celibacy and explains it as follows:[1]

> "*Abrahma* is an act of copulation arising out of sexual desire. *Hiṃsā* is inevitable in sexual intercourse as many vitalities are injured at the time of copulation."[2]

In this way it can be said that desire for sexual intercourse causes *bhāva hiṃsā* and any copulation leads to *dravya hiṃsā*.[3] Ācārya Samantabhadra explains it and says that one should not visit another person's wife and should remain contented with his own wife.[4]

There are five kinds of transgressions of this vow too:[5]

(i) *smaratīvrābhinivesa* — intense desire for sexual intercourse.
(ii) *anaṅgakrīḍā* — unnatural sexual indulgence.
(iii) *anyapariṇayakaraṇa* — arranging marriage of others.
(iv) *aparig hītatarayorgamana* — association with immorally married woman.
(v) *itvarikagamana*—going to an unmarried woman.

Parigrahatyāgāṇuvrata (Vow of Non-possession)

It is explained as *mūrcchā* or hallucination of possessions. It is

1. *Householder's Discipline in Jainism,* p. 43.
2. *Ibid.*
3. *Śrāvakācāra,* p. 69.
4. *Householder's Discipline in Jainism,* p. 89
5. *Ibid.*, p. 44.

divided into two types, e.g. *antaraṅga* and *bahiraṅga*.[1] This vow is also called as *parigraha-parimāṇa-vrata*. It is also explained as putting to one's own desire regarding worldly things, e.g. money, grains under a certain limit.[2]

There are various facts of this *vrata*. It is not possible here to explain all these facts of this *vrata*.

In this context it is necessary to present *aticāra*s of this vow. There are five transgressions of this vow.[3]

1. *kṣetra-vāstu pramāṇātikramaṇa*—exceeding limits of house and land from their existing shape.
2. *hiraṇya-suvarṇa-pramāṇātikramaṇa*—exceeding the limits of gold and silver ornaments.
3. *dhana-dhānya pramāṇātikramaṇa*—exceeding the limits of wealth, cattle and cow.
4. *dāsa-dāsī-pramāṇātikramaṇa*—exceeding the limit of man, women, servant.
5. *kūpya-bheda-pramāṇātikramaṇa*—exceeding the limits of clothes and utensils.

Rātribhojanatyāga

It is an additional vow of *aṇuvrata*s. For becoming pious a householder should discard eating during night. There are various insects seen and unseen which may die or be killed in the process of taking food during night. Therefore, a householder should abstain from eating during the night. In this way householder should renounce with mind, body and speech as *hiṃsā* is enevitable there.[4]

Now we come to *guṇa-vrata*s. There are three *guṇa-vrata*s, e.g. the *dig-vrata* or *sīla,* the *desaprimāṇa vrata* or *sīla,* the *anarthadaṇḍatyāga vrata* or *sīla*. All these above three are described here in order.

1. *Householder's Discipline in Jainism*, p. 45.
2. *Śrāvakācāra,* p. 73.
3. *Householder's Discipline in Jainism,* pp. 46-47.
4. *Ibid.,* p. 47.

The Dig-virati Sīla

It is made with two terms, e.g. *dig* and *virati*. *Dig* means direction and *virati* signifies keeping away from. This *dig-virati* refers keeping away from different directions. Referring about this it is said that—"In actual practice it refers to the choosing of a limited area for one's activities, as less as possible, out of the vast area of the world."[1] According to Samantabhadra this vow should be taken as follows: "I shall not travel beyond these limits of the ten directions"[2] it is determined like this with a view to avoiding *aṇu-pāpa*—minor sins for the rest of one's life. These directions are north, south, east, north-east, south-east, north-west, south-west, up and down. The *sāvaya-paṇṇatti* considers a householder like a heated iron ball. His movement can bring *hiṃsā*.[3]

There are five transgressions of this morality:[4]

1. *Ūradhvadikpramāṇātikramaṇa* (Exceeding the limit fixed for upward direction).
2. *Adhodikpramāṇātikramaṇa* (Exceeding the limit fixed for downward direction by descending into a well or cellar).
3. *Tiryagdikpramāṇātikarmaṇa* (Travelling in any of the eight directions beyond the fixed limits).
4. *Kṣetra-v ddhi* (Extending the limits for freedom of movement).
5. *Sm tyantaradhāna* (Crossing the set limits through forgetfulness).

Desavrata or Disaparimāṇasīla

This is the second vow of the three *guṇa-vrata*s. It can be called as supplementary to the *dig-virati sīla.*[5] In this vow a person take a resolution in a certain time that he will not proceed beyond a certain

---

1. *Householder's Discipline in Jainism,* p. 49.
2. *Śrāvakācāra,* p. 84.
3. *Ibid.,* p. 85.
4. *Householder's Discipline in Jainism,* p. 49, also in this book, p. 89: *Ūrdhamadhastāttiryakvyatikaramaḥ-kṣetrav dhirādhānaṃ*|
Sm tyantarasya gaditāḥ-pañceti prathamīlasya||
5. *Householder's Discipline in Jainism,* p. 50.

village and marketplace, etc.[1] The philosophy behind this vow is that a person should take a resolution in certain time not to visit a village, market, street or house. In this way he can practice more *ahiṃsā*.[2]

There are five breaches (*aticāras*) of this vow too which are as follows:[3]

1. *Presya-payoga*—Asking someone to work outside the limit.
2. *Ānayana-prayoga*—Sending for someone from beyond the fixed limit.
3. *Śabdānupāta*—Making sound or giving hints to those who are outside the limits to get certain works done.
4. *Rūpānupāta*—Making signs or gesture or any particular indication beyond limits so that a work can get be done.
5. *Pudgalakṣepaḥ*—Asking someone to throw something beyond the limits do that some works can be performed.

Anarthadaṇḍatyāgasīla

It is the third *guṇa-vrata*. Under this *vrata* a householder takes a resolution to abstain from harmful activities that do not serve any useful purpose.[4] Ācārya Samantabhadra defines it as, "Abstaining from wanton or purposeless activity which is likely to cause injury to others, within the determined limits."[5] Ācārya Samantabhadra has divided this vow into five kinds. Ācārya Am tacandra has divided this vow into six parts. These are as follows:[6]

1. *Apadhyāna*—It involves hunting, victory, defeat, adultery, theft, etc. A householder should avoid all these.
2. *Pāpopadesa*—A householder should not give harmful

---

1. *Jainism in Buddhist Literature,* p. 102.
2. *Householder's Discipline in Jainism,* p. 50.
3. *Ibid.,* p. 50; It can also be seen in the verse which is mentioned at the page no. 189 of this book.
   Presasya saṁparayojanamānayanaṁ- śabdarūpavinipātau|
   Kṣepopi pudgalānaṁ-dvitīyasīlasya pañceti||
4. *Śrāvakācāra,* p. 89.
5. *Ibid.*
6. *Householder's Discipline in Jainism,* pp. 51-52.

advice to anyone.

3. *Pramāda-caryā*—A householder should abstain from purposeless and mischievous activities.
4. *Hiṃsādāna*—A householder should remain careful with knife, poison, fire, plough, sword, bow, etc., used for injurious acts.
5. *Duḥśruti*—A householder should remain aloof from false and bad stories that excites passion, etc.
6. *Dūtakrīḍa*—It refers to gambling.

This *sīla* has also five transgressions which are as follows:[1]

1. *Kandarpa*—Poking fun at another
2. *Kautkucya*—Mischievously gesticulating or buffoonery.
3. *Bhogānarthakya*—It refers to the misuse of articles of use.
4. *Asamīks Maukhara*—It stand for non-sensical and purposeless gossip.
5. *Asamīkṣitādhikaraṇa*—It refers to any act which is done thoughtlessly.

Here it is important note that in *Śrāvakācāra,* term used for *bhogānarthakya* is the *upabhogāparibhogānarthakya.*[2]

Śikṣāvratas

There are four vows under this. These are *sāmāyika*, *prosadhopavāsa*, *bhogopabhoga*, and *atithisamvibhāga sila*.

Sāmāyika Sīla

It is derived from the word *samaya.* The word *samaya* can be broken into two parts, e.g. *sama* and *aya*. The meaning of the word *sama* is eqanimity or tranquillity of mind. The word *aya* refers to

---

1. *Tattvārthasūtra,* VII. 32. Here I owe this reference to *Śrāvakācāra,* p. 92. It can also be seen in the following verse which is in *Puruṣārthasiddhyupāyḥ,* p. 59. Here I owe this reference to *Householder's Discipline in Jainism.*
Kandarpaḥ kautkucyaṁ-bhogānarthakyamapi ca maukharyaṁ I
Asamīkṣitādhikaraṇam-t tīyasīlasya pañca iti II
2. *Śrāvkācāra*, p. 92.

attainment. Thus attainment of equanimity of mind is called *samaya.*[1] Explaining it Am tacandra says, "by giving up *rāga-dveṣa* affection and repulsion and, i.e. observing equanimity in all objects, one should practice *sāmāyika* continuously, which bring about the realization about the true nature of the self."[2] It is also explained also as the positive way of submerging the various activities related with body, mind and speech in the self (*ātman*).[3] It is also said that this *sīla* should be performed by sitting or standing at a tranquil place.[4]

There are five transgressions (*aticāras*) of this vow. These are as follows:[5]

(i) *mano-duṣpraṇidhāna*—misdirection of mind.
(ii) *vāg*[6]*-duṣpraṇidhāna*—misdirection of speech.
(iii) *kāya-duṣpraṇidhāna*—misconduct by body.
(iv) *anādara*—lack of interest in performing the vow.
(v) *sm tyānuprasthāna*—forgetting the required formalities.

Prosadhopavāsa Sīla

This *vrata* is very essential in performing *sāmāyika vrata.* It is said that to strengthen the daily practice of *sāmāyika vrata* a person should fast twice during each fortnight.[7] About this it is also said that after renouncing all household work one should take fast on eighth and on the fourteenth day of each lunar fortnight. Regarding fast it is said that one should commence fasting at midday preceding the *prosadha* day.[8] Then he should go to a secluded place and should meditate.[9]

---

1. *Householder's Discipline in Jainism,* p. 53.
2. *Ibid.*
3. *Rajavārtika,* VII. 21/7. Here I owe this reference to *Śrāvakācāra,* p. 93.
4. *Jainism in Buddhist Literature,* p. 103.
5. *Tattvārthasūtra,* VIII. 33, Here I owe this reference to *Śrāvakācāra,* p. 97.
6. In *Householder's Discipline in Jainism* it as *vacana,* p. 54.
7. *Householder's Discipline in Jainism,* p. 55.
8. *Śrāvakācāra,* p. 99.
9. *Ibid.*

The *sāvaya-paṇṇatti* refers four categories of application of *prosadha.*[1] Those are as follows:

(a) *āhāra-posaha*—in respect of food.
(b) *sarīra-sakkāra-posaha*—in respect of bodily care.
(c) *baṁbha-posaha*—in respect of celibacy.
(d) *vāvāra-posaha*—in respect of worldly occupation or activating.

Here it is necessary to say something about the *aticāra* (transgression) of this vow. It is enumerated as five:[2]

(i) *grahaṇāticāra*—acceptance of articles of adoration or worship without examining and handling them carefully.
(ii) *visargāticāra*—placing objects or spreading one's body on the ground without scrutinizing it.
(iii) *astaraṇāticāra*—preparing one's bad without carefully examining and harmlessly sweeping the place.
(iv) *anādarāticāra*—showing no interest or enthusiasm in observance of the fast.
(v) *asmaraṇāticāra*—forgetting the due procedure of the fast.

Bhogopabhogaparimāṇa Sīla

It is made with the word *bhoga* and *upabhoga*. *Bhoga* refers to these articles which are used only once like food, garlands, beetle, etc. *upabhoga* signifies those articles which can be used again and again, e.g. cots, ornaments and cloths, etc. This vow signifies the limitation in the use of objects of *bhoga* and *upabhoga* in order to minimize attachments to the objects.[3] The noted Ācārya Samantabhadra advises that a thing may be renounced for the whole life which is called as *yama*. In contrast to it a thing should be renounced for a limited period is called *niyama.*[4]

---

1. *Ibid.*, p. 100.
2. *Ratnakaraṇḍaka Śrāvakācāra,* v. 110; I owe this reference to *Śrāvakācāra,* p. 101.
3. *Householder's Discipline in Jainism,* p. 57.
4. *Householder's Discipline in Jainism,* p. 57.

Explaining this vow, it is said that by renouncing the articles of *bhoga* such as vegetable and articles made by milk several insects die because these are birthplaces of numerous *jīva* (beings).[1] By renouncing non-prohibited objects attachment is neutralized.[2]

The transgressions (*aticāras*) of it are as follows:

1. *sacittāhāra*—eating articles having life.
2. *sacittamisrāhāra*—eating articles mixed with those having life.
3. *sacittasambandhāhāra*—eating articles which are associated with those having life.
4. *duspākvāhāra*—eating articles not well cooked.
5. *abhisava*—eating articles that are prepared by fermentation.[3]

Atithisaṃvibhāga Sīla

This is the fourth *sikṣāvratas*. It is made up with *atithi* and *saṃvibhāga*. *Atithi* means guest. *Saṃvibhāga* means to share, part or division, etc. Therefore, this *vrata* is related with that should be shared with guests, etc. Here this *vrata* has a significant meaning. The meaning of the word *atithi* is ascetic or *sādhu*.[4] Therefore, to share with the guest the word *dāna* is used for this *vrata*.

There are various facets of this *vrata,* e.g. manner of donation, seven qualities of the donor, quality of food to be offered, grades of recipients and merits of giving donation, etc.[5] Here the manner of donation is given which is of ninefold.[6]

1. *saṃgraha*—respectful welcome.
2. *uccasthāna*—offering high seat.
3. *pādodaka*—washing the feet.

---

1. *Ibid.*
2. *Śrāvakācāra*, p. 102.
3. *Pururṣārthasiddhyupāyaḥ* V. 193, I owe this reference to *Śrāvakācāra,* p. 90.
   Āhāro hi sacittaḥ-sacittamisracittasambandhaḥ I
   Duspakvobhisavopi-ca pañcāmi saṣṭhasīlasya II
4. *Śrāvakācāra,* p. 104.
5. *Householder's Discipline in Jainism,* pp. 59-60.
6. *Ibid*., p. 59.

4. *arcanā*—worship
5. *praṇāma*—bowing.
6. *vākśuddhi*—purity of speech.
7. *kāya-śuddhi*—purity of body.
8. *manaḥ-śuddhi*—purity of mind.
9. *eṣaṇā-śuddhi*—purity of food.

Like other vow this *vrata* has also five kinds of *aticāra*s (transgressions).[1] Which include:

(i) *paradāt vyapadeśa*—It refers to the nation of articles belonging to others in one's own name.
(ii) *sacittanikṣepa*—placing the food on *sacitta* (i.e. articles having life in them).
(iii) *sacittāpadhāna*—giving articles those are covered with *sacitta*.
(iv) *kālātikramaṇa*—serving the articles at an improper time.
(v) *mātsarya*—giving donations with a jealous mind.

There are various merits of giving donations, e.g. overcoming of greed, renunciation from violences, etc.[2]

Sallekhanā

It has not been elaborated much by Śvetāmbara *ācārays*. There is some treatment in *Navapada-prakaraṇa* of Devagupta. In contrary to Śvetāmbara tradition the Digambara tradition has given much attention to this *vrata*. Famous Digambara Ācārya Āsādhara has treated *sallekhanā* well in his work *Sagaradharmā ta*. According to Samantabhadra–

> "The abandonment of the body on being confronted with unavoidable calamity, famine, senility and disease for the

1. *Householder's Discipline in Jainism,* p. 60, also it can be seen in the verse of the same book, p. 90:
Paradāt vyapadesaḥ-sacittanikṣepatatpidhāne ca |
Kālasyātikramaṇaṁ–mātsaryaṁ cetyatithidāne ||
2. *Ibid.*, p. 60.

> sustenance of religio-spiritual practices (*dharmāya*) is regarded as *sallekhanā*."[1]

The other terms which are used for *sallekhanā* are *samādhi-maraṇa* and *samyā-maraṇa*. In Kaṇṇaḍa it is also called as *sanvasana*.[2] The *sallekhanā* is also explained as a calm resignation and unruffled preparedness for meeting death.[3] According to *Puruṣārthasiddhyupāyaḥ*—"the only which would enable one to carry his wealth of piety with him is *sallekhanā*".[4]

Regarding *sallekhanā* it is said that it is not *samādhi*. *Sallekhanā* should also not be equated with suicide. Am tacandra concludes *sallekhanā* all passions which are the cause of violence are subdued, and hence *sallekhanā* is said to be leading towards *ahiṃsā*".[5]

Coming to this point it is necessary to say something about transgression of *sallekhanā*. It is of five kinds:[6]

1. *Jīvitāsaṃsā*—desire to live
2. *Maraṇāsaṃsā*—desire to die
3. *Suh dānurāga*—attachment towards friends
4. *Sukhānubandha*—revival of past pleasure
5. *Sanidāna*—explanation of future prosperity.

At this point it is necessary to present daily recitations of Jainas, which is as follows:[7]

The Namokāra Mantra

(i) *Namo Arahaṃtāṇaṁ*—Obeisance to the *arahanta*s (Perfect Souls)

---

1. *Śrāvakācāra*, p. 113.
2. *Ibid.*, p. 114.
3. *Householder's Discipline in Jainism*, p. 61.
4. *Ibid.*
5. *Ibid.*
6. *Ibid.*, p. 62. also in a verse from on p. 90:
   Jīvitamaraṇāṃsase-suhu dānurāgaḥ sukhānubandhas ca|
   Sanidānaḥ pañcaite-bhavanti sallekhanākāle||
7. Religion and culture of the Jaina.

(ii) *Namo Siddāṇaṁ*—Obeisance to the *siddhas* (Liberated Souls)
(iii) *Namo Airiyāṇaṁ*—Obeisance to the Masters (Head of Congregations)
(iv) *Namo Uvajjhāyāṇaṁ*—Obeisance to the Teachers (Ascetic Teachers)
(v) *Namo loe savva ashu ṇaṁ*—Obeisance to all the Ascetic Aspirants in the Universe.

After this it becomes necessary to talk about duties of a householder as reflected in Pāli literature.

Duties of a Jain Householder as Reflected in Pāli Literature

The *Samaññaphalasutta of Dīghanikāya* refers to fourfold bond of Nigaṇṭha Nāṭaputta. But here it is not clearly mentioned about the duty.[1]

Asibandhakaputta Gāminī was a Jaina follower. He was a Jaina householder. In response to a question he answers the Buddha that Nigaṇṭha Nāṭaputta teachers about four vows. A householder to remain vigilant from the following evil-doer:[2]

1. One who kills (*pāṇaṁ ati pāteti*)
2. One who steals (*adinnaṁ ādiyati*)
3. One who tells lie (*musā bhanati*)
4. One who indulges in sensual pleasures (*kāmesu micchācarati*). It is further said that he goes to purgatory (*so apāyiko nerayiko*)

A reference to five vows of Jainism is found in the *Aṇguttaranikāya*. Here five ways of falling into sin as taught by Nigaṇṭha Nāṭaputta can be seen as follows:[3]

1. Destruction of living beings (*pāṇātipātī hoti*)
2. Takes what is not given (*adinnādāyī hoti*)
3. Enjoys sensual desires (*abrahmacārī hoti*)

1. *Jainism in Buddhist Literature*, p. 94. It is instance of *Saṁyuttanikāya*.
2. *Ibid.*, p. 95.
3. *Jainism in Buddhist Literature*, p. 95.

4. Speaks lie (*musāvādī hoti*)
5. Takes liquor and intoxicants (*surāmerayamajjapamādaṭṭhāyī hoti*).

Another example can be seen from the *Majjhima Nikāya.*[1] Here Dīghatapassi of Nālandā with Buddha and says that Nigaṇṭha Nāṭaputta does not emphasize so much on *karma* but he gives importance to *daṇḍa*.

In this way instances of householders of Jainism can be seen in the Pāli *Tipiṭaka*.

Following are the important principles of Jainism:[2]

(i) The seven *tattvārtha*s
(ii) Substance, Qualities, Modes (*dravya, guṇa, paryāya*)
(iii) The Five *astikāya*s and *kāla*
(iv) Ekāntavāda and Syādvāda.

All these principles are one way or the other related to morality (*sīla*). Without *sīla* one cannot get *kaivalya* the summum bonum of Jainism.

1. *Jainism in Buddhist Literature*, p. 97.
2. Illuminator of Jain Tenets, pp. XIII to XXXIV of introduction.

4
Sīla as Precondition to Enlightenment

The ultimate goal of Buddhism is the attainment of *nibbāna*. The final goal of Jainism is attainment of *kaivalya*. It is the central point around which all types of activities are performed. A person observes the prescribed moral principles known as *sīla*. He practices the *samādhi* and realizes and visualizes *paññā* for attainment of *nibbāna*. As the steps of mountain lead towards its peak, so all the practices lead towards *nibbāna*. As all rivers flowing in different directions tend towards the ocean to merge into it, similarly all the teachings of the Buddha lead towards *nibbāna* and find consummation in realization of it. In Jainism all the types of *sīla vrata*s are directing to *kaivalya,* the final goal of Jainism. The Buddha established the fourfold assemblies, e.g. the assembly of monks, the assembly of nuns, the assembly of *upāsaka* and the assembly of *upāsikā*. The Jainas also have four kinds of assemblies. They are *sādhu, sādhvī, upāsaka* and *upāsikā*. The Buddha prescribed different types of moral and social rules to regulate the life of monks and nuns which have been mentioned in the *Pāṭimokkha*. The life of householders is regulated through the norms given by Buddha time and again and can be found in his discourses like *Maṅgalasutta, Vasalsutta* and, *Parābhavasutta*, etc. All the discourses make the life of monks and nuns perfectly pure and the consciousness also becomes serene, calm and quite. It becomes immensely pure and free from pollutions. This type of realization is called *nibbāna*. Thus it is said *sabbamala virahitaṁ accantaparisuddham... nibbānaṁ veditabbaṁ.*[1]

The word *nibbāna* has been interpreted in many ways at different places. It has two component parts, e.g. *ni* and *vāna*. *Ni* is a prefix with

1. *Vis., Sīlaniddesa,* (V.R.I.), p. 3.

negative implications. *Vāna* means desire. Therefore, *nibbāna* means, total negation of desire. Thus it is said that *taṇhāya vippamuttassa natthi soko kuto bhayaṁ.*[1] It can also be described from the root *bā* that means to blow out. *Nibbāna* indicates the blowing off. When the lamp of life process is blown off, it is called *nibbāna.*[2]

The five aggregates are regarded as *vana,* the forest. These are so called because these are associated with *upādāna* and called *upādānakkhandha*. When the *upādāna* is negated, absolutely annihilated and put to an end, that state is called *nibbāna*. It refers to the *pañcakkhandha* in its pure form. The word *vāna* refers to an arrow or thorn. As the thorn pierces into part of the body of living beings, so the immoral state pierces into the beings and disturbs him like anything and puts him under the dominating force of suffering. When this thorn of pollution of defilements is totally removed from *pañcakkhandhā,* the freedom is achieved which is called as *nibbāna*. In this way the meaning of the word *nibbāna* can be illustrated etymologically. It has also its traditional meanings that can also be understood in the light of the following references.

In the *Mahāvaggapāli* the Buddha is shown under the *bodhi* tree after attainment of the Buddhahood. It is shown there that the basis of his newly gained attainment of knowledge is the Law of Dependent Origination.[3] There and there alone, he is shown in expressing clearly that this is the process of becoming which leads to the process of suffering. There is also the process of getting rid of suffering which is the attainment of *nibbāna*. For this purpose he has clearly stated the relevance of the Law of Dependent Origination. This doctrine shows the process of becoming and also the process of getting rid of it. So one goes on becoming from one existence to another again and again and suffers. When he finally puts an end to the process of becoming, there is the attainment of *nibbāna*. Then, how becoming (*bhava*) continues to birth (*jāti*) is explained in the following way:

1. Depending upon ignorance, there arises volitional actions (*kamma* formation) (*avijjā paccayā saṅkhāra*).

---

1. *Dh., Piyavagga,* (V.R.I.), p. 40.
2. *St. N., Ratanasutta,* (V.R.I.), p. 120:
   Te khīṇbīja aviruḷhiccandā, nibbānti dhīrā yathāyaṁ padīp.
3. *Mahā, Mahākhandhaka,* (V.R.I.), p. 16.

2. Depending upon volitional actions, there arises consciousness (*saṅkhāra paccayā viññānaṁ*).
3. Depending upon consciousness, there arises conditional mental and physical phenomena (*viññānaṁ paccayā nāmarūpaṁ*).
4. Depending upon mental and physical phenomena, there arises the six faculties (*nāma-rūpa paccayā saḷātanaṁ*).
5. Depending upon the six faculties, there arises touch or sensorial and mental contact (*saḷātanaṁ paccayā phasso*).
6. Depending upon the contacts, there arises feeling (*phassa paccayā vedanā*).
7. Depending upon feeling, there arises desire (*vedanā paccayā taṇhā*).
8. Depending upon desire, there arises conditioned clinging (*taṇhā paccayā upādānaṁ*).
9. Depending upon clinging, there arises the process of becoming (*upādāna paccayā bhavo*).
10. Depending upon the process of becoming, there arises birth (*bhavapaccayā jāti*).
11. Depending upon birth, there arises decay, death, lamentation, and suffering (*jātipaccayā jarāmaraṇaṁ*, etc.).

It is called the *anuloma-paṭiccasamuppāda*.[1] This speaks about the process of going on of the repeated existences. There is also a reverse order of the Law of Dependent Origination that Buddha pondered for three times in the night. It is very important because the reverse order of the Law of Dependent Origination points out how the process of becoming can be put to an end. The aforesaid twelve links maintain the process of becoming. If one is eradicated, the other will be naturally eradicated. How it could be done? It is said that when the first is broken, the second will naturally be broken and so is the case with the others. When all the twelve links are broken, there is the stopping of this entirety of suffering (*asesa dukkhakkhandhassa nirodho hoti*).[2] The reverse order of the doctrine in brief is as follows:

---

1. *MN.*, *Mūlapaṇṇāsaka, Mahātaṁhāsaṅkhayasutta, Mahāyamakavagga,* (V.R.I.), p. 332.
2. *S.N.*, *Paṭiccasamuppādasutta, Nidānavagga, Nidānasaṁyutta,* (V.R.I.), vol. I, p. 2.

1. From the utter fading away of and stopping of this ignorance comes the stopping of volitional actions—habitual tendencies (*avijjāytveva asessavirāga nirodhā saṅkhāra nirodho*).
2. From the stopping of the volitional actions—habitual tendencies, there is the stopping of consciousness (*saṅkhāranirodhā-viññāna nirodho*), etc.
3. From the stopping of birth, old age, death, grief, sorrow and lamentation, suffering, dejection and despair are stopped. In this way, the entire mass of suffering (*dukkhahandha*) is stopped for ever.

Ignorance (Avijjā)

Hereafter describing the Law of the Dependent Origination, it is apt to say few words about the twelve *nidāna*s or the links. The first one is the *avijjā,* literally meaning not knowing. It has not been used here in this literal sense. It has its technical meaning. It is the darkness of ignorance that makes the mind bewildered and prevents understanding the nature of reality. It is called *avijjā* by its nature that *dhamma sabhāva paṭicchādana lakkhaṇā avijjā*[1] which means *avijjā* has the characteristics of covering the nature of reality. In its technical sense it is the name of not understanding the Four Noble Truths, moral and immoral roots and the Law of Dependent Origination. Under the binding influence of *avijjā* the nature of reality as impermanent and subject to suffering and substanceless is not understood. Since a man does not understand the nature of reality, he does various types of moral and immoral deeds. Therefore, it is said that depending upon *avijjā* there arises the *saṅkhāra*s.[2]

Mental Formation (Saṅkhāra)

The word *saṅkhāra* means activities or formation. It refers to the moral and immoral activities. In technical sense, it is called *puññābhi-saṅkhāra, apuññābhi-saṅkhāra,* and *āneñjābhi-saṅkhāra.* The *puññābhi-saṅkhāra* refers to the threefold moral activities. The

---

1. *Nettivibhāvinīṭīkā, Paṭiniddesavāra ātthavibhāvanā,* (V.R.I.), p. 224.
2. *MN., Bahudhātukasutta, Anupadavagga, Uparipaṇṇāsapāli,* (V.R.I.), p. 110.

puññābhi-saṅkhāra refers to the threefold immoral activities.[1] The *āneñja-saṅkhāra* stands for the mental and immoral activities. In short, all *saṅkhāras* stand for twenty-nine moral and immoral activities. Therefore, the *saṅkhāras* are the various types of activities done by people being influenced by the binding influence of ignorance. When an action is performed there is the appearance of the resultant. Any action done in any moment of life, yields a resultant.[2] It goes on accumulating and those resultants become the base of a new life. Therefore, there appears the *viññāna*.

Consciousness (Viññāna)

The word *viññāna* means consciousness. It is its literal meaning. It has also the technical meaning and that is the *paṭisandhi-viññāna* or the consciousness which unite the being from one existence to another. It is the name of the resultant consciousness responsible for rebirth. In clear term, it is the emergence of any one of the nineteen types of consciousness which gives *paṭtisandhi*.

Mind and Matter (Nāma-rūpa)

When a being is united in normal process in the way of *paṭisandhi,* immediately after that there appears the subtle form of mind and matter (*nāma* and *rūpa*). Here the word *nāma* stands for psychic factors and *rūpa* stands for basic material qualities and generated material qualities. The basic material qualities means for *mahābhūtas* and the generated material qualities means twenty-four *upādārūpas*.[3] They appears at this stage in very subtle form.

Sense Organs (Salāyatana)

It means six sense organs, namely, eye, ear, nose, tongue, touch and mind. They appear as our door of senses. These doors receive information of various objects through them.

1. *SN., Nidānavagga, Parivīmaṃsanasuttaṁ,* (V.R.I.), vol. 1, p. 74.
2. *Vis., Kaṅkhāvitaraṇavisuddhi, Paccayapariggahakathā,* (V.R.I.), pp. 236-37.
3. *Abhidhammatthasaṃgaha, Rūpa Paricchedo,* (V.R.I.), p. 43.

Contact of the Sense Organs (Phassa)

As soon as there is arising of the six senses, there starts the contact of the sense organs with the objects. It is the mere touch of the object with the sense organ. It may be the contact of the eye and the visible object, or the ear and the audible object and so on.

Feeling (Vedanā)

In common parlance *vedanā* is understood as suffering. It refers to feeling. When there is contact of the sense organs with the object, there arise the feelings due to that. Generally, it is of three types, pleasant feeling (*sukha-vedanā*), unpleasant feeling (*dukkha-vedanā*), and indifferent feelings (*upekkhā-vedanā*). Again the pleasant feeling is divided into two, as mental pleasure (*somanassa vedanā*) and physical feeling (*sukha-vedanā*). The unpleasant feeling is also of two types, namely, mental unpleasant feeling—(*domanassa-vedanā*) and physical unpleasant feeling (*dukkha-vedanā*). Indifferent feeling always remains mental.[1]

Desire (Taṇhā)

It means desire. It is the desire for worldliness. There are things surrounding a man and he develops attachment for them. We have desire for our belonging, property and, their maintenance, etc. Therefore the desire to reborn, *bhavataṇhā* wtih *sassata diṭṭhi*. We have also desire for the sensual pleasure, that is *kāma*. We have desire for the liquidator or terminator of being born again that is *vibhavataṇhā* with *uccheda diṭṭhi*. Thus the *kāma-taṇhā, bhava-taṇhā* and *vibhava-taṇhā* include the three types of major desires as explained by the Buddha.

Grasping (Upādāna)

It means strong urge to grasp or hold fast. When the urge becomes powerful and starts functioning through the different sense doors, it is called *upādāna*. Due to this, man takes sticks (*daṇḍa*) to hit

1. *MN., Sammādiṭṭhisutta,* (V.R.I.), p. 61.

others or uses harsh words (*pharusā vāca*), etc.

Existence (Bhava)

It literally means existence. The technical meaning is the lust for existence. It means doing again some moral and immoral deeds and accumulating the moral and immoral outcomes or kārmic force. Thus *bhava* means activities. This is *saṅkhāra*.

Birth (Jāti)

It means birth or *paṭisandhi*. It refers to the *viññāna* or the resultant consciousness which is reappearing in the form of a new life again (*nibbatti abhinibbatti khandhānaṁ pātubhāvo*).[1]

Decay and Death (Jarā-maraṇa), etc.

It means decay, wasting and death. Where there is *paṭisandhi,* the law of reality starts functioning and there also starts the decay, various kinds of sufferings and the end, dissolution and death. Here one should understand that the destruction is not the final end. It is the destruction and dissolution of the present process. Technically, one becomes *bhava* again and undergoes the process of rebirth (*jāti*) and experiences various types of pleasant and unpleasant feelings till one realizes *nibbāna*.[2]

While propounding the Law of Dependent Origination, Buddha took into consideration, the three forms of existence, the past, the present and the future. *Avijjā* and *saṅkhāra* refer to the past existence, *jāti* and *jarā-maraṇa* refers to the future existence and eight links between the two refers to present existence. It is in this way that depending upon the past, there arises the present and depending upon the present, there arises the future. In the *Visuddhimagga* it has been described according to *kamma* theory:

Atīta hetavo pañca-idāni phala pañcakaṁ |
Idāni hetavo pañca-āyatiṁ phala pañcakaṁ ||[3]

---

1. *Vibhaṅgapāli, Paṭiccasamuppādavagga, Aññamaññacatukkaṃ,* (V.R.I.), p. 160.
2. *AN., Tikanipāta Nidānasutta,* (V.R.I.), p. 160.
3. *Vis., Khandaniddesa,* (V.R.I.), p. 212.

It is in this way that there is the arising of one depending upon the other. All the twelve links are inter-dependent. If one is broken, the other is naturally broken. Thus in one way, it explains the process of becoming and in another way, it explains how it can be put to an end.

Then what is the bearing of the Law of the Dependent Origination on the concept of *nibbāna*? It may be seen in the statement of the Buddha. While explaining the various types of suffering, the five aggregates with grasping (*pañca-upādānakkhandha*) are explained as subject to suffering.[1] So when there is the association of *upādāna* (strong desire for grasping) with five aggregates, there is the continuance of suffering. What is the truth of such association with five aggregates? The truth lies in understanding the twelve links and the unbroken chain of continuity of the repeated existence. Therefore Buddha had stated the process of continuity of twelve links and the end of the process of existence. He also told that with the destruction of one link, there is the destruction of others. In this way, the gradual development of the defilements as well as the elimination of various types of defilement, impurities come to an end. When there is no defilement or impurities at all, the consciousness becomes immensely pure, and this state of pure consciousness free from all pollutions, is called *nibbāna*.[2] In this background, the concept of *nibbāna* should be examined. In the *Udānapāli* a very clear statement has been made by Buddha that just as the great ocean which has only one taste, that is of salt, similarly the *dhamma* and *vinaya* presented by him has only one taste and that is the taste of liberation[3] (*ekameva raso, vimuttiraso*).

Further, this is also stated by the fact that all rivers like Gaṅgā, Yamunā, Sarabhū, etc., flowing in different directions go to the ocean in the end, they all merge into it. Similarly all the discourses given by Buddha are linked towards *nibbāna*. It this background, the teachings, of the *Vinaya-Piṭaka* also have the same taste of liberation. It is called *vimutti-rasa*.[4]

---

1. *DN., Mahāvaggapāli, Mahāsatipaṭṭhānasutta, Dukkhasaccaniddesa*, (V.R.I.), p. 228.
2. *Vis., Sīlaniddesa, Nidānakathā,* (V.R.I.), p. 3.
3. *Udānapāli, Soṇavagga, Uposathasutta,* (V.R.I.), p. 129.
4. *Samantapāsādikā, Nidānavagga, Bāhiranidānavaṇṇanā,* (V.R.I.), p. 4.

The expression of *nibbāna* has appeared in various forms in the *Mahāvagga*. Buddha names it as *amata* (nectar). What is this nectar? It is the state where death (*maraṇa*) disappears for ever and immortality remains. The being goes beyond the region of death. The *Mahāvaggapāli* describes *nibbāna* as a state of *amata*.[1] While addressing the Brahmā Sahampatī, Buddha says, opened are the doors of immportality—*apāpuretaṁ amatassa dvārāṁ*.[2] What is needed to be done has been done (*kataṁ karaṇīyaṁ*).[3] Another explanation of the *nibbāna* is seen in the course of dialogue between Buddha and the Upaka *ājīvaka*. First of all it appears as *sīti bhūtosmi nibbuto*. The Buddha says that I have been immensely calm by realizing *nibbāna*. Referring about His motive of journey of Kāśī, He stated that he was going to beat the drum of *am ta* in the world that had been made blind due to ignorance. Thus it appears as *andhabhūtasmiṁ lokasmiṁ, āhañchaṁ amataduṁdubhiṁ.*[4]

The expression about the attainment of *nibbāna,* is seen with reference to the first discourse given by the Buddha to the fivefold monks. It appears with four attributes. They are the process of birth *khīṇājāṭi,* is over; the holy life is led, *vūsitaṁ brahmacariaṁ,* what was to be done,—*kataṁ karinīyaṁ* that there is no further coming to the world *nāparaṁ ithatthāyāti*.[5] Thus these expressions of *nibbāna* are very significant, when it is said that *khīṇājāti,* it speaks aout putting an end to *saṁsāra*. What is *saṁsāra – saṁsarati iti saṁsāro*. It is the case

> *Khandhānaṁ paṭipāti, dhātu āyatanānica* I
> *Abbhocchiṇṇaṁ vattamānaṁ saṃsāroti pavuccati* II[6]

The combination of five aggregates, twelve ways and eighteen elements without any interruption is called *saṃsāra*.[7] Therefore, the word *khīṇājāti* makes it clearer that the process of existence is over.

---

1. *Mahā., Mahākhandhaka, Sāriputtamoggallanapabbajjākathā,* (V.R.I.), p. 46.
2. *Mahā., Mahākhandhaka, Brahmāyacanakathā,* (V.R.I.), p. 7.
3. *DN., Sīlakkhandavagga, Sāmaññaphalasutta,* (V.R.I.), p. 74.
4. *Mahā., Mahākhandhaka,Pañcavaggiyakathā,* (V.R.I.), p. 11.
5. *M.N., Mūlapaṇṇāsaka, Bhayaberavasutta,* (V.R.I.), p. 29.
6. *Vis.*, (V.R.I.), p. 173.
7. *Ibid.*

It is seen here that two words are always together, i.e. *vusitaṁ brahmacariyaṁ*. Here the *brahma* means noble, the sublime and *cariya* is the way of life. Therefore, the *brahmacariya* means the noble way of life. How is it done so? Because, it prescribes a path with noble states of purification, known as *sīla*, *samādhi* and *paññā*. *Sīla* is the base of holy life that appears in the form of a set of moral conducts whereby the physical and vocal activities are controlled.[1]

Samādhi means concentration or one-pointedness of the mind.[2] It (*kusalacittaekaggata-samādhi*). It states the process of developing concentration on an object whereby the mind becomes calm and serene. All the factors which make the mind restless are subdued, suppressed and made functionless.

By Jhāna factors like initial application of mind on the object (*vitakka*), sustained application of mind on the object (*vicāra*), a thrill of pleasant sensation (*pīti*), composure (*sukkha*) and one-pointedness (*samādhi* or *ekaggatā*), the mind gets concentration. Gradually the four *rūpajhāna* and four *arūpajhānas* are achieved. With that his mind becomes pure, subtle and pliable and with such a mind he understands the threefold characteristic of the nature of reality. Knowing so, he curtails the attachment and realizes *nibbāna*. It is in this sense that this is called *kataṁ karaṇīyaṁ*, etc.[3] This is the process of attainment of *nibbāna*. As the attainment of state and its process does have references available in the *Vinaya Piṭaka,* so simply it is said that Buddha attained *nibbāna*.

In course of time we find the names of the gradual state as *sotāpatti-magga-sotāpatti phala, sakadāgāmi magga-sakadāgāmi phala, anāgāmi magga-anāgāmi phala, arahanta magga-arahanta phala*.[4]

The *Vinaya Piṭaka* gives a few stories, how a person becomes an enlightened one, by attaining *nibbāna* and by cutting of all evils.

There were five *arahanta – pañcavaggiyā bhikkhū* in the beginning of Buddha's mission as it had been told earlier. Añña Koṇḍañña was the first convert. His attainment of *sotāpatti* is described as follows:

Añña Koṇḍañña having seen *dhamma,* attained *sotāpatti*, knew

---

1. *SN., Sagāthakavagga, Brāhmaṇasaṃyutta, Jatāsutta,* (V.R.I.), p. 192.
2. *Milindapaña,* (V.R.I.), p. 36.
3. *SN., Khandasaṃyutta, Arahantasutta,* (V.R.I.), p. 77.
4. *DN., Pāṭhikavagga, Saṅgītisutta,* (V.R.I.), p. 201.

dhamma, plunged into *dhamma* having crossed over doubt, having put away uncertainty, having attained without another's help to full confidence in the teachers' instruction. He spoke thus to the Lord: "May I receive ordination". These versions in the texts are almost the same for newcomers and also in getting the first eye of Truth (*sotāpatti*).[1]

Here it is necessary to examine the nature of getting rid of impurities (*kilesa*) in gradual attainment of the goal of the path towards *nibbāna* for *sekha.*[2] Those who have gained the first eye of the truth (*sotāpattī*), path (*magga*) and fruits (*phala*), *sakadāgāmī,* path and fruits, *anāgāmī* path and fruits and those who have gained the *arahanta* path (*magga*) belong to this category, called *sekhā*s as they are under training to attain *nibbāna*. It the stages of the path and fruits (*magga, phala*) there are two moments. In the stage of path, he cuts the fetters and in the stage of fruit, he knows that they have been broken. The former is the moment of action and the latter is that of realization. Here in the *sotāpatti* stage the fetters of a belief in a soul (*sakkāyadiṭṭhi*), doubt (*vicikicchā*) and believe in rites and rituals (*sīlabbataparāmāsa*) are eliminated. When they are once uprooted, then they never come. A large amount of unwholesome (*akusala-dhamma*) and their results are also eliminated with them.[3]

The extent of the *akusaladhamma,* thus eliminated, should be clear from the statement of Buddha wherein He has said that the remaining *akusala-dhamma*s are equivalent to the bit of soil on his toe and those liquidated are equivalent to the soil on the whole of the earth.[4] Brāhmaṇa Kūṭadanta for example was guilty of the most heinous evil deeds connected with wrong view (*micchādiṭṭhi*), and also of observing the ritual sacrifices, etc., where hundreds of animals were to be killed. These *akusala-dhamma*s were powerful enough to send him to hell (*niraya*). However, Kūṭadanta attained the stage of *sotāpatti* after meeting Buddha and listening to his preaching. Most of the *akusala-dhamma*s, accumulated earlier were also eliminated with his attainment of the stage of insight into truth (*sotāpatti*).[5]

---

1. *SN., Mahāvagga, Saccasaṃyutta, Dhammacakkappavattanasutta,*(V.R.I.), p. 487.
2. *MN., Majjhimapaṇṇāsaka, Gahapativagga, Sekhasutta,* (V.R.I.), p. 22.
3. *St. N., Ratanasutta,* (V.R.I.), p. 120.
4. *DN., Sīlakkhandavaggapāli, Kūtadantasutta,* (V.R.I.), p. 132.
5. *Ibid.*

The person who succeeds in realizing the path and the fruit of Once-returner (*sakadāgāmi-magga* and *sakadāgāmi phala*) does not completely eradicate any other fetters in addition to those eradicated at the *sotāpatti* stage, but he weakens the passion (*kāmarāga*) and hatred (*paṭigha*). In the moment of path, he makes them weak, and in the moment of fruit he knows that they have been made weak.

As a result of this reduction, further functioning of these immoral states with their results is eliminated. Here it may be marked that the *sotāpanna* is reborn for seven times, the *sakadāgāmi* is born for only once. After being born in a superior world, he returns once to the human world to attain *nibbāna*. Thus the reduction of possible births is as a result of the elimination of a large amount of kārmic power in the stage of *sakadāgāmi*. In this context, it is said that the person who was not reduced the lower fetter (*orambhāgiya saṃyojana*), for him, the fetters that give further births (*uppattipaṭlābha-saṃyojana*) and the fetters that extend existence (*bhavapaṭilābhasaṃyojana*) still remain.[1]

The person known as *anāgāmi* eradicates completely the two fetters—passion (*kāmarāga*), and hatred (*paṭigha*) which were already weakened, in addition to the other three eliminated at the *sotāpātti*-stage.[2] Here also in the moment of path, he eradicates and in the moment of fruit, he knows that they have been eradicated. Due to total destruction of these two fetters he never returns to this world but is born spontaneously (*opapātika*) the *brahmaloka* known as *suddhāvāsa brahmaloka* and attains *nibbāna* there. He has thus eliminated all the *kamma*s capable of giving birth in world of passion (*kāmaloka*).

Pukkusāti who attained the stage of *anāgāmi* after listening to Buddha's preaching met with an accident and died before joining the order. The Buddha then said that he would be born spontaneously in a *brahmaloka* and would attain *nibbāna* there.[3]

The person who has realized the path to *arahanta* stage (*magga*) also belongs to the *sekha*-category, since he is still under

---

1. *AN.*, *Catukkanipātapāli, Puggalavagga, Saṃyojanasutta,* (V.R.I.), p. 153
2. *SN.*, (V.R.I.) *Khandavaggapāli, Khandasaṁyutta, Aniccasutta,* p. 20.
3. *MN.*, (V.R.I.) *Uparipaṇṇāsapāli, Vibhaṅgavagga, Dhātuvibhaṅgasutta,* p. 287.

training. The person who has realized the fruit of *arahanta* (*phala*), is no more *sekha*, as he has completed his training.[1]

The distinction between paths (*magga*) and fruits (*phala*) is extremely subtle and tradition gives eight categories of perfection having divided the four stages into paths (*magga*) and fruits (*phala*).[2]

Venerable Aññā Koṇḍañña was the first person who obtained insight into the Truth (*sotāpatti*). Moreover, while the first discourse was being uttered, the mind of the group of five monks was also freed from the defilements and grasping. At that time, there were six perfected ones (*arahantas*) in the world.[3]

An *arahanta* has eliminated both *kusala* and *akusala kamma*,[4] (*puññapāpapahīṇassa natthi jāgarato bhayaṁ*[5]) as well as their generating results – (*paṭisandhi, viññāna*) and sporadic results (*pavatti, vipāka*). An *arahanta* reaches the height by following the moral activities, practising concentration and realizing the wisdom (*vipassanā*) except the higher achievements of the *pacceka buddha* and the *buddha*. The defiling factors are totally destroyed. The five higher fetters are also uprooted. The ties of becoming are broken for ever and he is free from all pollution.

The five fetters destroyed in the end are as follows:

1. Craving for fine-material existence (*rūparāga*),
2. Craving for immaterial existence (*arūparāga*),
3. Conceit (*māna*)
4. Restlessness (*uddhacca*),
5. Ignorance (*avijjā*).[6]

It is said that the *arahanta* also breaks the kārmic force capable of giving any further birth, through the three circles:

1. The Circle of *kamma—kamma-vaṭṭa*

---

1. *Vis., Sīlaniddesa, Sīlappabhedakathā,* (V.R.I.), p. 4.
2. *DN., Pāṭhikavagga, Pāsādikasutta,* (V.R.I.), p. 98.
3. *Mahā., Mahākhandaka, Pañcavaggiyakathā,* (V.R.I.), p. 19.
4. *St. N., Mahāvagga, Sabhiyasutta,* (V.R.I.), p. 162.
5. *Note:* Some people describe wholesome deeds make the *saṃsāra* long. But there is no such idea in this doctrine.
6. *Pṭṭhā, Saññojanagocchakaṃ, Vibhaṅgavāra,* (V.R.I.), vol. p. 1.

2. The Circle of defilements—*kilesa-vaṭṭa*
3. The Circle of results—*vipāka-vaṭṭa*.

After eradicating these three circles no *kamma* remains. Hence, he is one who has eliminated all wholesome and unwholesome *kammas*. Further, through the extinction of all cankers – (*āsavakkhaya*), he has reached in this very life the deliverance of mind, the deliverance through wisdom and thus is free from cankers. He has himself understood and realized as a fully and wholly perfected one. This is the state of *nibbāna,* realized in this stage of existence.

Another aspect in the process of attainment of *nibbāna* is seen in the *Mahāvaggapāli* in the story of the son of rich householder Kolivisa of Campā.[1]

It runs as follows. When the Buddha was dwelling in the city of Rājagaha, Soṇa Kolivisa came to the Buddha and obtained ordination. Having received instructions he was walking up and down there and doing meditation (*caṅkamana bhavana*) in the Sītavana grove with a firm determination. When he was repeating it, his feet were injured; the place became covered with blood, like a slaughter-house. Thereupon a thought came to his mind and he said to himself: "Let me now, return to the lower state (*hīnāyāvatteyya*), enjoy my wealth and do good deeds."

The Buddha perceived it within his mind, the thought of venerable Soṇa, came and He discussed the same with him. He questioned Soṇa as "Now what do you think Soṇa: You were skilled, were you not at the lute's stringed music when formerly you were a householder?" "Yes Lord," replied Soṇa.

"What do you think about this Soṇa? When the strings of your lute were too tight, was your lute at that time tuneful and fit for playing?"

"Not, indeed Lord". "What do you think about this Soṇa?" "When the strings of your lute were too loose had your lute then any sound, was it in a fit state to be played upon?" "No indeed Lord." "What do you think about this Soṇa?"

"When the strings of your lute were neither too much stretched nor too loose, but fixed in even proportion, had your lute played

---

1. *Mahā., Cammakkhandhaka, Soṇassapabbajjā,* (V.R.I.), pp. 251-52.

well?" "Was it then in a fit state to be played upon?" "Yes, Lord". "Just to Soṇa, does too eager a determination does conduce to self-righteousness, and too weak a determination to sloth.

Do thou, therefore, O Soṇa, be steadfast in and the oneness of determination, press through to harmonize your mental power. Let that be the object of your thought."

"Even so, Lord", the venerable Soṇa answered the Buddha in assent.

Thence forward, the venerable Soṇa was steadfast in the evenness of determination. He pressed through to harmonize his mental powers, and took it as the object of his thought.

And the venerable Soṇa remaining alone and separate, earnest, zealous, and resolved, attained ere-long to that supreme goal of their higher life (*brahmacariya*), for the same of which noble youths go forth from all and every household gain and comfort to become homeless houseless wanderers—that supreme goal did he, by himself, and while yet in this visible world, bring himself to the knowledge of, and continue to realize, and to see face to face.[1]

And he understands clearly that rebirth is at an end, the higher life has been fulfilled, all what should be done had been accomplished and that after this present life there would be no rebirth. So Soṇa became another among the perfected ones (*arahanta*s). After this Soṇa paid a visit to the Lord Buddha, and bowed down before him and described his attainment "As whatsoever *bhikkhu*" said the Lord, is an *arahanta* whose inflexes (*āsava*s) are rooted out who had lived the life, who has accomplished the task, who has laid aside every burden, who has gained the end, he had in view, who has quite broken the fetter of craving for further existence, who is completely set free by insight, six things doth: 1. He reaches up – unto renunciation, 2. Unto the love of solitude, 3. Unto kindness of heart, 4. Unto the destruction of grasping, 5. Unto the destruction of craving, and 6. Unto getting free from delusions.[2]

"Thus, Lord even if shapes cognizable by the eye come very strongly into the field of vision of a monk whose mind is wholly freed, they do not obsess his mind, comes to be underfilled, firm, won to composure and he notes its passing hence." If sounds

1. *Mahā., Cammakkhandhaka, Soṇassapabbajjā*, (V.R.I.), pp. 251-52.
2. *Ibid.*

cognizable by the ear, if scents cognizable by the nose, if tastes cognizable by the tongue, if touches cognizable by the body, if mental objects cognizable by the mind come very strongly into the thought of a monk whose mind is wholly freed, they do not obsess his mind, for his mind remains undefiled, firm, won to composure, and he notes its passing hence."[1] Here, the importance of meditation through the story of the venerable Arahanta Soṇa is seen. It is advised, therefore, that the calm concentration (*samatha bhāvanā*) and insight meditation (*vipassanā bhāvanā*) should be developed while following the eightfold path (*ariya aṭṭhaṅgika magga*), and thereby there shall be the achieving of *nibbāna*.[2] Here *samatha* (tranquillity) meditation prepares the mind for *nibbāna, vipassanā* meditation unfolds the nature of reality for realization of *nibbāna*.

The practitioner (*yogāvacara*) while doing *vipassanā* meditation on the objects like the object of impermanence (*aniccā*), the object of dissatisfaction or suffering (*dukkha*), the object of soulnessness (*anatta*), attains *nibbāna* in one of the three ways, as the emptiness – deliverance (*suññatā vimokkha-nibbāna*), the conditionless deliverance (*animitta vimokkha nibbāna*), the desireless deliverance (*appaṇihita vimokkha nibbāna*).[3]

Then what is the characteristic feature of *nibbāna*? There is nothing worldly pleasure like that of joy in *nibbāna* but its pleasure is coolness, freedom, happiness, non-craving, non-thirst and *vimutti sukha*, etc.[4]

The *Suttanipāta* also describes *nibbāna* as *chandarāga vinodānaṃ nibbāna pada muccatain*.[5] The word *vimutti-sukha* is used to explain the *nibbāna*. The *Bahuvedaniyasutta* in the *Majjhimanikāya* and *Dīghanikāya* describe the word *sukha* as it is used not for ordinary joy but for freedom from craving.[6]

What is it then? It is freedom from whole *dukhakhanda*, therefore it is *vimutti-sukha*. If the *nibbāna* is an absolute external repose, it would come to mean as a permanent attainment. As it has been explained earlier, Buddhist does not believe in a soul. It clearly

---

1. Mahā., *Cammakkhandhaka, Soṇassapabbajjā,* (V.R.I.), pp. 251-52.
2. *MN., Mūlapaṇṇāsaka, Dhammadāyādasutta,* (V.R.I.), p. 20.
3. *Vis.*, (V.R.I.), vol. 2, p. 299.
4. *St. N., Pārāyanavagga, Upasīvamānavapucchā,* (V.R.I.), p. 237.
5. *St.N., Pārāyanavagga, Hemakamānavapucchā*, (V.R.I.), p. 239.
6. *MM., Majjhimapaṇṇāsaka,* (V.R.I.), p. 69.

teaches that it has only mind and matter (*pañcakkhandha*) which has been discussed in respect of Dependent Origination (*paticcassamuppāda*). Buddha rebutted the ideas of soul as described in the *Brahmajālasutta* as sixty-two wrong views.

Further, not only the Hindus believe but also the Christians and Muslims believe in a powerful creator God. This has been further discussed in the book *The Religious Experience of Mankind* as "while Christian and Muslim mystics see their own higher experiences as being a kind of contact or union with God, the Buddha did not interpret his own enlightenment as such".

The *Māghasutta* in the *Suttanipāta* explains that there is no becoming of an *arahanta* after his death (*yesaṁ gatī natthi idha-vippahāya*).[1] The essence of Buddhism regarding beings is that there is only mind and physical body (*pañcakkhandha*), but nothing else. Therefore, after the death of an *arahanta* there is neither rebirth nor any permanent element left behind.

Buddha in the *Upasīvamānavapucchā* and the *Ratanasutta* in the *Suttanipāta* has replied to the question raised by a few, including *Upasīvamānava,* regarding the permanence of soul. He explained as when a light goes out, the direction cannot be stated to which it has gone—*accī yathā vātavegena khitto*[2] and *nibbanti dhīrā yathāyaṁ padīpo*.[3] This idea has also been found expressing in the same manner in the Sanskrit *Saundarānanda Mahākāvya* of Bhadanta Ashvaghosha.

When an *arahanta* dies, his dead body decays that is all and nothing more. It cannot be said as to where the being has gone. However, it can be said that the Buddhist *nibbāna* is not an annihilation (Ucchedavāda). When we consider about it in the background of Aggivacchagotta and Māluṅkaputta's conversation with the Buddha in *Salāyatanavagga* of the *Saṁyuttanikāya* as well as the *Upasīva-mānavaka pucchā*—in the *Suttanipāta*; one can have a clear understanding of the Buddhist position in connection to the theory of annihilation. The Buddha refutes eternalism (Sāsvatavāda) as well as annihilation (Ucchedavāda). *Nibbāna* is neither related to Sassatavāda not to Ucchedavāda. It has been described as *asaṅkhatattha*—uncreated, beyond of all becoming and

1. *St.N. Mahāvagga, Māghasutta,* (V.R.I.), p. 156.
2. *St.N., Pārāyaṇavagga, Upasīvamānavapucchā,* (V.R.I.), p. 237.
3. *St.N., Cūḷavagga, Ratanasutta,* (V.R.I.), p. 120.

conditionally (*nissaraṇaṭṭha*), overcoming by deliverance (*pahāna*), *vivekaṭṭha*—having rest in detachment. Here detachment has been called as of following two types:

1. Bodily detachment (*kāya viveka*), and
2. Mental detachment (*citta viveka*) deathlessness from repeated death (*amataṭṭha*).[1]

Nibbāna on this account is borne without reason. So there is no reason to produce *nibbāna*.

In contradiction to this all the beings and things are created by cause or conditions (*saṅkhāta*). All the animate and inanimate things are always changeable and impermanent. The five aggregates cease to exist after attainment of *parinibbāna*. In the state of *sa-upādisesa-nibbāna,* they become pure.

The *arahanta* who attains *nibbāna* does not undergo annihilation or attains a state of union with a permanent soul after his death. *Nirodha* does not mean cessation of *nibbāna* but the cessation of craving hence becoming and birth. *Nibbāna,* therefore, destroys causes of becoming (*samudāya*) and annihilation at the same time.[2]

In the *Upasīvamānavapucchā* of the *Suttanipāta,* Brāhmaṇa Upasīva questions Buddha whether the state of *arahanta* is a permanent state or undergoes annihilation after death. Buddha replies that there remains nothing of the *arahanta* after his death, because he attains a state which goes beyond reasons and logic.[3] It can only be said that he has attained the state of *nibbāna* but what is that state, remains beyond the reach of expression.

According to the *Munisutta,* the *arahanta* is free from immoral deeds. At the same time, even he does something moral, it does not produce a resultant. He goes beyond the force of *kamma*.[4] So he lives here in this world till his death in a state of indescribable joy going beyond permanence and annihilation. The Buddha did not reply the question as to what would happen to him after his *parinibbāna,* because thc state is beyond the power of expression (*avisaya*).[5]

---

1. *Dha., Bālavagga, Vanavāsītissasāmaṇeravatthu,* (V.R.I.), Vol. I.
2. *Vis., Indriyasaccaniddesa, Nirodhaniddesakathā,* (V.R.I.), p. 136.
3. *Thera., Dasamavagga, Vijayattheragāthā,* (V.R.I.), p. 181.
4. *St.N., Urgavagga, Munisutta,* (V.R.I.), p. 116.
5. *Ibid.*

Nibbāna may not be a mere psychological fact. The cessation of craving and ignorance (*taṇhā* ana *avijjā*) is not empirical, in the ordinary sense, as it cannot be explained by psychology or any other science.

The state of *nirodhasamāpatti* bears in evidence to this fact. An *arahanta* who has gained eight *samāpatti,* can live for one week long in *nirodhasamāpatti* without a mental process but with only physical stillness.[1] His body contains heat (*tejodhātu*), when he gets up from this state, he wakes up with *arahanta phala-citta*.[2] This proves that it is a state of happiness or *arahanta* in his lifetime and not mere a psychological fact. The Buddhist tradition maintains higher consciousness as eight trances (*aṭṭhasamāpatti*) and five types of intuition (*abhiññā*) in the mundane level. *Nibbāna* is the highest consciousness at supra-mundane level (*lokuttara*). In other words it is the supreme knowledge—*āsavakkhaya-ñāna*. Thus *nibbāna* may be described as absolute spiritual fact to be realized within by following the Noble Path in the background of soullessness. When we consider another aspect of *nibbana*, there are two forms of *nibbānadhātu,* namely, *sa-upādisesa-nibbānadhātu* and *anupādisesa-nibbānadhātu*.[3] *Upādi* means five aggregates. When the five aggregates become free from all the defiling factors, they remain as *pañcakkhandha* and not as the *pañca-upādānakkhandha*. There is the existence of the five aggregates but in the pure and unpolluted form. It means the *yogāvacāra* attains a state of *arahanta*-hood free from the snare of attachment. He realizes the joy of emancipation. The *anupādisesa nibbānadhātu* is a state of *nibbāna,* where the five aggregates cease to exist. It does not mean that they reach the state of annihilation (Ucchedavāda), but rather they come to the state of complete rest, a state beyond the verbal expression. This takes place after the death of the *arahanta* and hence technically explained as *parinibbāna*.

Buddha, in the *Udānapāli* has thrown light on the nature of *nibbāna*. He explains that there is *nibbāna,* which is not born, not seen, not done and not arisen by reasons.[4]

---

1. *SN., Nidānavaggapāli, Dhātusaṃyutta, Sattadhātusutta,* (V.R.I.), p. 133.
2. *Ibid.*
3. *M.N., Uparipaṇṇāsaka, Devadahavagga, Suṇakkhattasutta,* (V.R.I.), p. 45.
4. *Udānapāli Pāṭaligāmiyavagga, Tatiyanibhānapatisaṃyuttasutta,* (V.R.I.) p. 165

Buddha says that there is a *āyatana* (base) which has neither this world, nor that world, nor origin, nor death, nor not origin.[1]

In the *Rohitassasutta* Buddha explains that *nibbāna* is realizable in this life when he exists with his body. He may realize the *loka* in the four ways as *imasmiṁ yeva byāmamattake kalebare lokañca paññapemi, lokasamudyañca lokanirodhañca lokanirodhagāminī patipadañca paññapemi.*[2] *Nibbāna* cannot be created (*asaṅkataṭṭa*). It is realized by the *yogāvacāra* by practising the Noble Eightfold Path (*ariyaaṭṭhaṅgikamagga*).

While replying to the King Milinda, Thera Nāgassena says that there is *nibbāna*, which is understood by wisdom with the higher knowledge (*ariyamaggañāna*).[3] This higher knowledge maintains that all things, material and non-material, exist only on the basis of mutual dependence of causes and effects which has been explained in the concept of Depedent Origination. Such understanding removes the heresies of the creator or destroyer, etc., when such nature of reality is understood, the attachment is curtailed and *nibbāna* is realized.

Nibbāna cannot be understood by mere logic.[4] *Nibbāna* is not nothingness or unreality. It is a reality or a fact of life. There is coolness and there is heat, there is darkness and there is light. Similarly when there is death, there must be non-death. That is *nibbāna* (*amata-pada*). This is realized within oneself, by one who is rightly set on the Noble Path.

When paid attention to the both of religions—Jainism and Buddhism it can be seen that a lot of similarities are there. They can be collected to one place for the convenience of the research.

The Buddha was from the Śākya family. The Mahāvīra was from the Jñātrik dynasty. Both of them belonged to kṣatriya clan. Buddha left the household life at the age of 29. Mahāvīra left the household life at the age of 30. Buddha toiled hard for near about six years and then became the fully enlightened one (*sammā*

---

1. *Udānapāli, Pāṭaligāmiyavagga, Tatiyanibhānapatisaṃyuttasutta,* (V.R.I.). p. 165.
2. *SN., Devaputtasaṃyutta, Rohitassasutta,* (V.R.I.), p.76.
3. *Milindapañha, Meṇdakapañha,* (V.R.I.), p. 143.
4. *AN., Catukkanipāta, Thānasuttaṁ,* (V.R.I.), p. 219.

sambuddha). Mahāvīra exerted for twelve years and then he came to be known as *Jina* (Conqueror).

After the Third Buddhist Council Buddhism truly became a world religion. It was Aśoka who really transported Buddhism from India to different parts of the world. Gradually Buddhism got its place in different parts of the modern world too. Jainism did not become so wide in comparison to Buddhism. But it did not loose its position as Buddhism lost in its place of origin. Jainism did not spread in the world like Buddhism. May be Jainism did not get a patron like Aśoka. Royal patronage played an important role in spread and consolidation for ground to Buddhism.

In the conclusion general similarities and dissimilarities of Buddhism and Jainism are presented.

Three Gems (Triratna) of Buddhism

1. Buddha
2. Dhamma
3. Saṅgha.

Three Gems (Ratna-traya) of Jainism

1. The Full Knowledge or Right knowledge (*samyag-jñāna*)
2. The Right Conduct (*samyag-cāritra*)
3.. Right Belief (*samyag-d ṣṭi* or *samyaktva*).

In Buddhism the three gems are given as highest signs of the religion. In *Mahānāmasutta* the Buddha explains those who take refuse in the triple gem they become Buddhist.[1] In other context it is said those who have taken refuse of Buddha, etc., are protected by the *dhamma* always.[2]

But at the side of Jainism these three gems are appearing as qualities. Right Knoledge means wisdom and understanding. Right Conduct represents the behaviour of the path and Right Belief represents one's emancipation.

---

1. *AN.*, *Aṭṭhakanipāta, Gahapativagga, Mahānāmasutta,* (V.R.I.), vol. 3, p. 55.
2. *Theragāthāpāli, Dhammikattheragāthā,* (V.R.I.), p. 212.

Personal Information about Buddha

1. Father—Suddhodana
2. Mother—Mahāmāyā
3. Wife—Yaśodharā
4. Birth place—Lumbinī
5. Cousin and Brother-in-Law—Devadatta
6. Son—Rahula
7. Horse—Kanthaka
8. Charioteer—Channa
9. The First Teacher—Āḷārakāḷāma
10. The Second Teacher—Uddakarāmaputta
11. The First Sermon—*Dhammacakkappavattana*
12. Left house at the age of—29
13. Clan—Śākya
14. Place of enlightenment—Buddhagayā (Bodh-Gayā)
15. Place of Mahāparinibhāna—Kuśīnārā.

Some Personal Information about Mahāvīra

1. Father—Siddhārtha
2. Mother—Triśalā
3. Wife—Yaśodā
4. Daughter—Jameli
5. Birth place—Kundagrāma near Vaiśālī
6. Left house at the age of—30
7. Clan—Jantrika
8. Place of enlightenment (*kaivalya*)—J mbhikāgrāma
9. Place of death—Pāvāpurī
10. Toiled hard for—12 years
11. Jain people believe him as—24th *tīrthaṅkara*.

In this list also there are a lot of similarities of the Buddha's and Mahāvīra's biographies. Siddhārtha was Buddha's lay name and it was the name of the father of Mahāvīra. Yaśodharā was the wife of Siddhārtha and Yaśodā was Mahāvīra's. Both left their household life at their 29 and 30 of age respectively. Siddhārtha toiled six years and Mahāvīra twelve years. Here we can investigate the appearance of their biographies in the following manner.

Some Aspects of Councils of Buddhism

Not only the point of doctrine and biography of these religious teachers, but their religious culture and history also have been improved in the same background. After Buddha's demise great disciples of Him established few types of council time to time with the patronage of certain kings. In the same way Jainas also assembled councils for the protection of dispensation.

1. *First Council*—It was convened by the patron Ajātasattu of Magadha under the chairmanship of Mahākassapa Mahāthera. It resulted in compilation of the *Tipiṭaka* in oral tradition. Technically it is called *pañcasatikā* because 500 *arahanta* monks took part in it.

2. *Second Council*—It was summoned at the patronage of King Kālāsoka. The venue of the council was Vālukārāma of Visālā. Technically it is called as *Sattasatikā*, because 700 *arahanta* monks took part in it.

3. *Third Council*—It was convened at the instigation of the King Aśoka. About one thousand monks took part in it under the chairmanship of Mogglliputtatissa Thera. Technically it is known as *Sattasattikā*, because 1,000 *arahanta* monks took part in it. It resulted in compilation of the text *Kathāvatthu*.

4. *Fourth Council*—It was convened in Puruṣapura in modern Peshawar in Pakistan under the chairmanship of Vasumitra under the patronage of King Kaniṣka.

Some other councils also took place in Buddhism but the above-mentioned four councils were arranged in India and are more prominent. Therefore, only four has been named here to show the similarities between these two religions.

Some Aspects of Councils of Jainism

1. *First Council*—This council was convened at Paṭalīputra by Sthūlabāhu in the beginning of the third century B.C.E. It resulted in the compilation of the 12 *aṅga*s (sections) to replace the lost texts of 14 *pūrva*s (former texts). Here it is important to note that this council was only accepted by the Śvetāmbaras.

2. *Second Council*—Held at Vallabhi in Gujarat in the fifth century C.E. only Śvetāmbaras took part in it under the leadership of Devaradhi Kṣamāśramaṇa. It resulted in final compilation of the 12 *aṅga*s and 12 *upāṅgas*.

Tīrthaṅkaras in Jainism

I. Ṛṣabha (Ādinātha)
II. Ajitnāth
III. Sambhavanāth
IV. Abhinandanāth
V. Sumatināth
VI. Padmaprabhā
VII. Supārśvanāth
VIII. Candraprabha
IX. Puṣpadanta
X. Śītalnāth
XI. Śreyānśanāth
XII. Vasupūjya
XIII. Vimalnāth
XIV. Vimalnāth
XV. Anantanāth
XVI. Dhammanāth
XVII. Śāntināth
XVIII. Kunthunāth
XIX. Aranāth
XX. Mallināth
XXI. Munisuvrat
XXII. Namināth
XXIII. Nemināth
XXIV. Pārśva
XX. Mahāvīra

Buddhas in Buddhism

I. Dīpaṅkara
II. Koṇḍañña
III. Maṅgala
IV. Śumana
V. Revata
VI. Sobhita
VII. Anomadassī
VIII. Paduma
IX. Nārada
X. Padumuttara

XI. Sumedha
XII. Sujāta
XIII. Piyadassī
XIV. Atthadassī
XV. Dhammadassī
XVI. Siddhattha
XVII. Tissa
XVIII. Phussa
XIX. Vipassī
XX. Sikhī
XXI. Vessabhū
XXII. Kakusandha
XXIII. Koṇāgamana
XXIV. Kassapa
XX. Gautama Buddha.

Not only these things but also, *vassūpagamana, dhutaṅga, vikālabhojanavirati* and some more similarities are coming in these two religions. All those activities and things are directed to both *nibbāna* and *kaivalya*.

To fulfil *śramaṇa dharma* or monkhood in Jainism there are ten kinds of qualities which are necessarily to be completed:

(i) *kṣamā*: forgiveness
(ii) *mārdava*: humbleness
(iii) *ārjava*: frankness
(iv) *mukti*:free from desires
(v) *tapa*: penance of twelve kinds
(vi) *saṃyama*: to stop all inflow of *karma*s
(vii) *satya*: truth, avoiding untruth
(viii) *sauca*: purity of conduct
(ix) *akiṃcanaya*: to abstain from wealth
(x) *brahmcarya*: celibacy.

Regarding this list of qualities we have to say that Buddhism also shows same things as its steps towards emancipation. Following is a comparison of above ten qualities and their usage in Buddhism.

kṣamā —This teaching is coming in Buddhism as *Khanti.*

natena paṇḍito hoti-yāvatā babu bhāsati
khemī averi abhayo-paṇḍitoti pavuccati[1]

mārdava and ārjava—

These teaching are çoming in following verse as *maddava* and *ajjava.*
Brahmacariyañca sīlañca-ajjavaṁ maddavaṁ tapaṁ
soraccaṁ avihiṁsañca-khantiñcāpi avaṇṇayuṁ[2]

mukti (*mutti*)

katamañca bhikkhave dukkhanirodhaṁ ariyasaccaṁ. yo tessāyeva taṇhāya asesavirāganirodho cāgo paṭinissaggo mutti anālayo.[3]

tapa (*tapa*)

idha nigrodha tapassi tapaṁ samāiyati, so tena tapasā attamano hoti paripuṇṇasaṅkappo.[4]

saṁyama (*saññama*)

uposathaṁ upavasissaṁ, sādu sīkesu samvutā
saññamā saṁvibhāgā ca, vimānaṁ avasāmahaṁ[5]

satya (*sacca*)

saccaṁ bhane na kujjheyya, dajjā appampi yācito
etehi tīhi ṭhānehi, gacche devāna santike[6]

śauca (*suci*)

imaṁ bhonto nisāmetha, abhirūpo brahā suci

---

1. *Dh.*, *Dhammaṭṭhavagga,* (V.R.I.), p. 46.
2. *St.N.*, *Cūlavagga, Brāmaṇadhammikasutta,* (V.R.I.), p. 128.
3. *DN.*, *Mahāvagga, Mahāsatipaṭṭānasutta,* (V.R.I.), p. 232.
4. *DN.*, *Pāṭhikavagga, Udumbarikasutta,* (V.R.I.), p. 30.
5. *Vimānavatthupāli, Itthivimāna, Uttarāvimānavatthu,* (V.R.I.), p. 12.
6. *Dh.*, *Kodhavaga,* (V.R.I.), V. 224, p. 41.

caranena ca sampanno, yugamattañca pekkhati[1]

akiñcanaya (*akiñcana*)

yassa pure ca pacchā ca, majjhe ca nattthi kiñcanam
kiñcanam anādānaṁ, tamaham brūmi brāhmaṇaṁ.[2]

brahmacarya (*brahmcariya*)

yam kiñci sithilaṁ kammaṁ, saṅkiliṭṭhañca yaṁ vatam
saṅkassaraṁ brahmacariyaṁ, na taṁ hoti mahapphalan.[3]

From the verses given above we can have a clear idea that Buddhist and Jaina doctrines have a lot of similarities between them. It can be due to the same social background and time in which Buddhism and Jainism took place in India.

It is clear that the ultimate goals of Buddhism and Jainism are the attainment of *nibbāna* or *kaivalya.* It is the central point around which all types of activities are carried on. A person observes the prescribed moral principles known as *sīla.* He practices the *samādhi* and realizes and visualizes *pañña* for attainment of *nibbāna*. As the steps of mountain lead towards its peak, similarly all the practices lead towards *nibbāna* or *kaivalya*. As all rivers flowing in different directions tend towards the ocean, to merge into it, similarly all the teachings of the Buddha lead towards *nibbāna* and find consummation in realization of it.

Buddha established the fourfold assemblies, the assembly of monks, the assembly of nuns, the assembly of *upāsaka* and the assembly of *upāsikā*. He prescribed different types of moral and social norms to regulate the life of monks and nuns which have been mentioned in the *Pāṭimokkha*. In the same way Jainism also proclaimed the vows and rituals for the *sādhus, sādhvī*s and lay disciples. The life of the householders is regulated by the norms given by Buddha from time to time in his discourses like *Maṅgalasutta, Vasala, Parābhavasutta*, etc. All these discourses make the life of

1. *St. N., Mahāvagga, Pabbajjāsutta,* (V.R.I.), p. 143.
2. *MN., Majjhimapaṇṇāsapāli, Vāseṭṭhasutta,* (V.R.I.), p. 419 and *Dhammapada,* V. 421, p. 65.
3. *SN., Devaputtasaṃyutta, Tāyanasutta,* (V.R.I.), p. 59.

monks and nuns extremely pure. Life becomes immensely pure and free from vices. This type of realization is called *nibbāna*. It is said in both these religions that without the practice of moral behaviour one cannot get *nibbāna* or *kaivalya* at all.

In this sense the concept of *sīla* in both religions is showing that morality is pre-condition of liberation, even though there are lot of differences in both religions due to their philosophical background. The concept of soul has been accepted by the Jainism but Buddhism does not accept it. The Jainas practice *sīla* as a *vrata*. They are very extremistic in nature when the matter of fulfilment of *vrata*s comes. Buddhism rejects the practice of *sīlabbataparāmāsa* (attach to a *sīla vrata*). In Buddhism *sīla* helps get *samādhi* (concentration) and *samādhi* helps get *paññā* (wisdom). That is why it is said that— *sīla paribhāvitā samādhi, samādhi paribhāvitā paññā*. The main goal of Buddhism is awakening of the wisdom. That is called as *vipassanā*. To attain *nibbāna, vipassanā* and *paññā* are essential. Under these circumstances *sīla* is given as the precondition to the enlightenment in both Buddhism and Jainism.

Conclusion

As stated in the beginning, the main objective of this research is to investigate into the moral philosophies and the moral codes in Buddhism and Jainism and to find out some valid criteria for a universal ethical system which is an essential requirement for the peace and unity of mankind in the modern world.

For the above purpose we have analysed and observed the morality (*sīla*) in Buddhism and Jainism in the second and the third chapters. The fourth chapter is devoted to clarify the importance of morality as a pre-condition to enlightenment.

Through the above-mentioned analysis and observation it has been found that Buddhism and Jainism agree with some universal factors regarding the moral behaviour of people in the modern world. Before embarking on it is important to summarize the moral philosophy and the nature of moral codes in both Buddhism and Jainism.

Regarding the Buddha's ideas on man and the universe, He teaches that the Dependent Origination is important. *Saṃsāra* is not spontaneously generated and there one cannot find an ever-lasting soul. In Buddha's presence a, *bhikkhu* named Sāti expressed his belief in the existence of a permanent *viññāna* (or soul). The Buddha explained to him that *viññāna* was based on cause and effect (*hetu-phala*). According to Law of Dependent Co-origination (*paṭiccasamuppāda*) when conditions that lead to a cause disappear, *viññāna* itself disappears. Buddhism maintains that actions (*kusala* and *akusala kamma*) which are generated from intention and the organic life which comes into existence on the basis of results of *kamma* are all fashioned by the process of the Dependent Co-origination. When the cause disappear results also disappear. This theory of Dependent Co-origination as well as some of the other characteristic features of the doctrine of the Buddha also have been discussed in the present work in the second chapter. It is very essential becauase so-called cycle of birth and death can be stopped by *sīla*, *samādhi* and *paññā*.

According to the idea of Jainism beings are bound to this life cycle with their old *karman*. So long as *karman* is not eradicated no body can be released from this birth and death. So he who wants to experience *kaivalya,* he should follow the path which is prescribed in the Jaina *dharma*.

There the practice of *sīla* is called as *vrata*s. They are mentioned in the third chapter in detail. If one looks at this word *vrata* according to the Buddhist point of view one may say that it deffers from the teachings of Buddha. But when one examines these *vrata*s carefully one can understand that most of these *vrata*s can be seen in Buddhism under the explanation of *sīla*. The extremist practices can be also seen in the Buddhism in the form of thirteen austerity practices (*terasa-dhutaṅga*). These *dhutaṅga*s are very similar to the Jaina *vrata*s.

Mind is very important in the both religions. In Buddhism to fulfil a *kamma* it should have done with intention (*cetanā*). Whether somebody does have intention to do, even it is not materialized, *kamma* is not doen. *Abhijjā, vyāpāda* and *miccādiṭṭhi* are called as the mental sins. However, to fulfil an *akusala-kamma* like, killing and stealing, etc., the required limbs should be completed. But regarding this Jainism teaches that there are *saṅkallpaja* or intentional injury. They are named as *sūkṣma-hiṃsā.* Some Jaina practitioners at least do not breath without using a mask (see Appendix 2 photos 13 and 14). Because they believe that small germs in the form of beings may die in taking breath. So according to Jainism *karma* can happen before talking or doing.

Similarly while travelling Jaina monks use a broom-like equipment to avoid insects and other living beings (see Appendix 2 photo 10). They do not take any chance to kill an insect even without intention. Not only towards the living beings but also to the trees and seeds their loving kindness can be seen. The same teaching is coming in Buddhism too. Once a brāhmaṇa Kāśībhāradvāja offered a bowl of milk-rice to Buddha. Buddha rejected that food due to some reasons and advised him not to throw it on grasses or in water minding the lives of insects (*appaharite vā chaddetha, appāṇake vā udake opilāpetha*). In the same way

Buddha advised not to cut the trees. Cutting trees is prohibited in *pācittiya* rules of the *Vinaya Piṭaka*.

To take moderate food is a good practice for everybody. It is a necessary practice for a monk both in Buddhism and Jainism. Buddha's advice in this regard is that one should not hanker for the food (*āhāre ca anissito*). He must take a limited amount of fod (*mattaññutā ca bhattasmiṃ*). There has been given to methods of limiting one's meal.

One should stop eating keeping space at least for four or five rice lumps. Second method is that one should take food to make an end of hunger but one should certainly not suffer by eating too much.

Similarly Jainism also prescribed not to make attachment with food. In Jaina practices the monks eat whatever they obtained. According to the lay society they have a lot of other aims of food. Not only to survival but also to keep skin smooth, body fit, keep the muscles in good condition, etc., as clergy both Buddhist and Jaina monks take their food only to conduct celibacy and survival of their lives.

Both the religions have their own meditational practices. To obtain the final goal in their systems both Buddhism and Jainism have given some meditational methdos. Of late, meditation is gaining popularity in society.

Shaving their heads is a requirement for Buddhist monks in the society (see Appendix 1 photos 5-8). There are variuos benefits of this. These have been discussed in *Milindapañha* during the conversation between Rohaṇa There and child Nāgasena. The details of this story have been discussed in this work. Jainism also prescribes the same practice. Mainly the Digambara monks follow this rule.

Buddhist monks use limited clothes. Buddha has given the permission to have only three robes for a monk. If he gets more than that he has to dispose it to the Saṅgha. If a monk keeps more than three robes for ten days without disposing it to the Saṅgha, he is breaking a rule (*nissaggiya pācittiya*). Buddha prescribed this *vinaya* rule because monks fall in trouble when they had a lot of robes. At the same time they might develop attachments to clothes. The story of Bāhubhāṇḍika Thera can be taken as a good example.

Regarding cloth Mahāvīra rejected to wear anything. Even today there are such kinds of naked *sādhus* in certain places in India

(Digambaras) (see Appendix 2 photos 17 and others). When the time passed some of the Jaina monks started to have white clothes. They are called as Śvetambaras. The idea of not having clothes means not to attach to any worldly matter. Both religions have the same idea but in different ways.

The Buddhist view of the world of experience is that everything is interrelated as causes and effects. The theory on which this view is based is called the theory of Dependent Co-orgination. Due to this reason everything in the world both mental and physical phenomena is impermanent. What is impermanent is unsatisfactory. What is unsatisfactory is essenceless or soulless. In order to get rid of this unsatisfactory nature of the world we have to follow a path leading to the cessation of unsatisfactoriness of suffering. The path includes three main stages as morality (*sīla*), concentration (*samādhi*) and wisdom (*paññā*). These three stages are divided into eight factors in detail:

(i) Right View (*sammādiṭṭhi*)
(ii) Right Thoughts (*sammāsaṅkappa*) – Wisdom
(iii) Right Speech (*sammāvācā*)
(iv) Right Action (*sammākammanta*)
(v) Right Livelihood (*sammā-ājīva*) – Morality
(vi) Right Effort (*sammāvāyāma*)
(vii) Right Mindfulness (*sammāsati*)
(viii) Right Concentration (*sammāsamādhi*) – Concentration

Through the development of right views and thoughts one can get a clear understanding of the world of experience which is a prerequisite for the journey towards the enlightenment. With this clear and right understanding based on the three characteristics, four noble truths and the theory of Dependent Co-origination one can begin his moral journey towards its end. The moral path in Buddhism begins with virtue (*sīla*) which includes the restrainment of physical and verbal behaviour and the right organization of livelihood. Then he proceeds to the third stage which includes the restrainment of mental behaviour through the development of right effort, right mindfulness and producing the trances.

As per the above-mentioned Buddhist path the first and foremost important fact is to get a clear view of the world of experience. It is an intellectual approach at the very beginning. This general understanding of the real nature of the world becomes one's own realization at the end of the path. At the beginning it may be identified as intellect (*buddhi*) and at the end of the path it should be called wisdom (*paññā*), liberation (*vimutti*) or emancipation.

Now it is very clear that the Buddhist path to liberation begins with morality. Morality means not only the external restrainment of physical and verbal behaviour of man. As Bhadanta Buddhaghoṣa defines, "the volition (*cetanā*), etc. of the person who is engaged in noble action and proper duties is called morality (*sīla*). The restrainment of external behaviour of man leads to the restrainment of mental behaviour which leads to the real understanding of the world. The wisdom so developed helps one to get rid of this mundane existence. So the morality in Buddhism is the basis for the enlightenment which is the final result of spiritual development and the one and only way to make an end to the mass of suffering related to birth, decay, illness, sorrow, etc.

Now we turn to the spiritual path and world view of Jainism. Jainism also considers this mundane world as a misery. The cause of misery is explained under two headings:

(i) Inflow of kārmic matter (*āsrava*) and
(ii) Bondage (*bandha*).

All activities, verbal, physical and mental cause the inflow of kārmic matter. If these activities are good they create happiness and if they are bad they turn to bad results. These are called *karman.* From the practical point of view the good activities are preferable to bad activities but from the real point of view both good and bad activities should be totally rejected because both of them create bondage of the soul to this world. According to Jainism the final liberation (*kaivalya*) means the total freedom of soul from this mundane world. Buddhism also prefers good actions (*kusala kamma*) as the basis of mundane happiness or social well-being here and hereafter. But as far as final liberation is concerned both good and bad should be rejected. As to Jainism the soul is kept bound with mundane world because of four kinds of passions:

(i) anger
(ii) pride
(iii) hypocrisy, and
(iv) greed.

The moral training is beneficial to annul the above passions. The Jaina theory of *karman* is very complexed and it is more extensive than that of Buddhism. In brief there are eight types of *karman* in Jainism:

(i) Knowledge — obscuring *karmans* (*jñānāvaraṇīya*)
(ii) Connotation — obscuring *karmans* (*darśanāvaraṇīya*)
(iii) Deludig *karmans* (*mohanīya*)
(iv) Destructive *karmans* (*antarāya*)
(v) Feeling — breeding *karmans* (*vedanīya*)
(vi) Family — determining *karmans* (*gottakarmans*)
(vii) Age — determining *karmans* (*āyuṣkarman*)
(viii) Body — determining *karmans* (*nāmakarman*).

The each and every *karman* is related to a set of activities. They are prescribed in Jaina *sūtra*s in detail. As to Jainism *karman* is a permanent force which can be eliminated only receiving their respective results. Buddhism also accepts a theory of *kamma* but it is totally based on psychological factors. *Kamma* in Buddhism is not a permanent entity outside the person who is responsible for it. So, the Buddhist path is sometimes introduced as the path leading to the cessation of *kamma*. After establishing the theory of *karman* as the cause of misery of Jaina scriptures recommend the method of its elimination under two headings:

(i) Stopping the inflow of fresh kārmic matter (*saṃvara*)
(ii) Annihilation of the kārmic matter already accumulated (*nirjarā*).

The means recommended for stopping the inflow of fresh kārmic matter are as follows:

(i) Threefold self-discipline (*trigupti*)
(ii) Fivefold path of vigilance (*pañcasamiti*)
(iii) Ten categorical qualities (*daśa-lakṣaṇa-dharma*)
(iv) Twelvefold reflections on the nature of the universe (*dvādasānuprekṣā*)

(v) Equanimous fortitutde of twenty-two hardships (*dvāviṃśati-parisahajeya*)
(vi) Five types of conduct (*pañcacāritra*).

The annihilation of already accumulated *karman* can be achieved by practising austerities. The austerities are divided into two as external and internal.

(i) external austerities:
  (i) fasting
  (ii) eating less than one's fill
  (iii) taking a secret vow to accept the food only if certain conditions, about which no one knows, are fulfilled.
  (iv) Renouncing delicacies
  (v) Sitting and sleeping in lonely place and
  (vi) Mortifying the body with mental equanimity.
(ii) The internal austerities are as follows:
  (i) expiation
  (ii) reverence
  (iii) service
  (iv) study
  (v) detachment and
  (vi) renunciation.

From the above analysis of the Jaina theory and spiritual path its main objective is the purification of soul from *karman*s. *Karman*s produced physically, verbally and mentally are connected with and motivated by passion. Passionate activities inflow into the soul and as a result sould is defiled and it cannot liberate itself from the misery. When the self is absorbed in its own intrinsic pure consciousness, shutting out the impure state of desire, aversion and delusion, the inflow of kārmic matter does not take place. It is an ideal stage.

Comparing both the moral philosophy and moral codes of Buddhism and Jainism we can clearly understand that both the religions despite minor differences agree with the following:

(i) Buddhism recommends a moral code for both the social

peace and harmony and the final libe 'tion through elimination of greed, hatred and delusion.

(ii) Jainism recommends a moral code for both the social peace and harmony and the liberation of soul from *karman*s related to desire, aversion and delusion.

Both the religions have an ideal of moral perfection as *nibbāna* and *kaivalya*. In Christianity and Islam the God is soemtimes interpreted as the ideal of moral perfection. So, as the basis of universal moral system we can propose an ideal status to be accepted by any designation such as the God, *nibbāna,* pure soul, or *kaivalya*. The greatest ideal of moral perfection is essential because all common people are not perfect beings. After accepting such a moral ideal all can agree on some common code of moral precepts with some minor changes in relation to the cultural, geographical and environmental factors. The leading force behind all such moral precepts is the ideal of moral perfection. According to our observation of moral codes of Buddhism and Jainism we can propose the five precepts as a set of moral precepts that can be universally accepted.

(i) Not to kill
(ii) Not to steal
(iii) Not to commit adultery
(iv) Not to lie
(v) Not to take intoxicating drinks.

These five precepts confirm,

(i) the security of life
(ii) the security of property
(iii) the security of family-life
(iv) the security of good name (fame) in the society, and
(v) the security of health respectively which are common needs of all kinds of people in the world.

And these five actions that is killing, stealing, etc., are prohibited by law universally with some conditions. These can be followed without inclination to any religion, creed, caste or country.

Further all religions can accept the moral training by following the five precepts as leading to social harmony, unity and peace as well as some day t moral perfection. It is to be mentioned that these five precepts are related to Christain and Islamic moral codes with minor changes. They also can be accomodated easily in the moral codes not only in other religions such as Hinduism, Taoism and Confucianism but also in the principles accepted by the Orgainization of United Nations.

Bibliography

PRIMARY SOURCES

Edition of Canonical Texts

Abhidhammatthasaṅgaha, ed. Bhadanta Revatadhamma and Ram Shankara Tripati, BVS, Varanasi, 1967; and also published by Vipassana Research Institute, Dhammagiri Igatpuri, India: First Edition 1998; co-publisher, The Corporate Body of the Buddha Educational Foundation, Taipei, Taiwan, and ed. Bhikkhu Bodhi; Tr. Mahathera Narada. *A Comprehensive Manual of Abhidhamma* (Sri Lanka: Buddhist Publication Society, 1999).

Aṅguttaranikāyo, 6 vols, VRI Dhammagiri-Pali Ganthamala, (Davanagari) 35, Igatpuri; 1995 1st edn. and also, ed. R. Morris & E. Hardy, 5 vols. (London: PTS, 1885-1900). Trans. F.L. woodward, vols. I, II, & V; E.M. Hare, vols. III and IV, *The Book of the Gradual Saying* (London: PTS, 1955-70).

Atthasālinī, Vipassana Research Institute, Dhammagiri Igatpuri, India: First Edition 1998; co-publisher, The Corporate Body of the Buddha Educational Foundation, Taipei, Taiwan and also, ed. P.V. Bapat and R.D. Vadekar, Fergusson College, Poona, First Edition (Poona, 1942) Bhandarkar Oriental Series No. 3.

Buddhavaṃsaṭṭhakahā, Hevavitarana Printing, Sinhala script, 1922, Mahabodhi Society of Sri Lanka. And also Vipassana Research Institute, Dhammagiri Igatpuri, India: First Edition 1998; co-publisher, The Corporate Body of the Buddha Educational Foundation, Taipei, Taiwan.

Buddhavaṃsapāli, Vipassana Research Institute, Dhammagiri, Igatpuri, India: First Edition 1998; co-publisher, The Coporate Body of the Buddha Educational Foundation, Taipei, Taiwan.

Dhammapadaṭṭhakathā, 2 volumes, published by Vipassana Research Institute, Dhammagiri Igatpuri, India: First Edition 1998; co-publisher, The Corporate Body of the Buddha Educational Foundation, Taipei, Taiwan and also 2 volumes, Hevavitarana Printing, Sinhala script, 1919, Mahabodhi Society of Sri Lanka.

Dhammapadapāli, Tr. K.T.S. Sarao, Munshiram Manoharlal Publishers Pvt. Ltd. Delhi, 1st edn. 2009 and also, Vipassana Research Institute, Dhammagiri, Igatpuri, India: 1st edn. 1998; co-publisher, The Corporate Body of the Buddha Educational Foundation, Taipei, Taiwan and also, tr. Narada Thera, published by Buddhist Missionary Society 123, Jalan Berhala, 50470, Kaula Lampur, (Malaysia, 1978 1st edn. 1963) also ed. & trans. Mahathera Narada (Calcutta: Mahabodhi Society of India, 1992).

Dīghanikāyao, ed. Mahesh Tiwary, Reading material series, University of Delhi publication, 1982 and also 3 vols. Published by Vipassana Research Institute, Dhammagiri, Igatpuri, India: First Edition 1998; co-publisher, The Corporate Body of the Buddha Educational Foundation Taipei, Taiwan and also, ed. Swami Dwarakā Dāsa Shastri, Baudha Bharati Series (Varanasi, 1996); Tr. T.W. and C.A.F. Rhys Davids, *Dialogues of the Buddha* Part I-III, Part I (London: PTS, 1992, 1st edn. 1899); Part II, (London: PTS, 1989, 1st. edn., 1910); Part III, (London: PTS, 1995, 1st edn., 1921).

Itivuttakaṭṭhakathā, Vipassana Research Institute, Dhammagiri Igatpuri, India: First Edition 1998; co-publisher, The Corporate Body of the Buddha Educational Foundation, Taipei, Taiwan and also Hevavitarana Printing, Sinhala script, 1919, Mahabodhi Society of Sri Lanka.

Jātakaṭṭhakathā, Vipassana Research Institute, Dhammagiri Igatpuri, India: First Edition 1998; co-publisher, The Corporate Body of the Buddha Educational Foundation, Taipei, Taiwan and also Hevavitarana Printing, Sinhala script, 1919, Mahabodhi Society of Sri Lanka.

Jātakapāli, Vipassana Research Institute, Dhammagiri, Igatpuri, India: 1st edn., 1998; co-publisher, The Corporate Body of the Buddha Educational Foundation, Taipei, Taiwan.

Khuddakapāthapāli, Vipassana Research Institute, Dhammagiri, Igatpuri, India: First Edition 1998; co-publisher, The Coporate Body of the Buddha Educational Foundation, Taipei, Taiwan and also, ed. B. Satyapala and Dr. Om Prakash Pathak, Bhikshu Satyapala, General Secretary, Buddhist Tri-Ratna Mission, New Delhi 1992.

Mahāvaggapāli, Vipassana Research Institute, Dhammagiri, Igatpuri, India: First Edition 1998; co-publisher, The Coporate Body of the Buddha Educational Foundation, Taipei, Taiwan and also, ed. Mahesh Tiwary, Reading material series, prepared and published by the Department of Buddhist Studies, University of Delhi, 1985.

Majjhimanikāya, ed. Mahesh Tiwary, published by the Department of Buddhist Studies, University of Delhi, 1983 and also 3 vols. and also, Vipassanan Research Institute, Dhammagiri, Igatpuri-Pāli Ganthamala, (1995 1st edn.) and also ed. V. Trenckner & R. Chelmers, 3 vols. (London: PTS, 1888-96). First trans. I.B. Honer, *The Collection of Middle Length Sayings,* 3 vols. (London: PTS, 1954-59). Second trans. Bhikkhu Nanamoli; trans., ed. & revised by Bhikkhu Bodhi. *The Middle Length Discourses of The Buddha* (Boston: Wisdom Publication, 1995).

Milindapañhapāli, Vipassana Research Institute, Dhammagiri Igatpuri, India: First Edition 1998; co-publisher, The Corporate Body of the Buddha Educational Foundation, Taipei, Taiwan, also ed. & tr. Swami Dwaraka Dasa Sastri BBS, Series-6 (Varanasi, 1990).

Nāmarūpapariccheda, Vipassana Research Institute, Dhammagiri Igatpuri, India: First Edition 1998; co-publisher, The Corporate Body of the Buddha Educational Foundation, Taipei, Taiwan.

Nettivibhāvinītīkā, Vipassana Research Institute, Dhammagiri Igatpuri, India: First Edition 1998; co-publisher, The Corporate Body of the Buddha Educational Foundation, Taipei, Taiwan.

Pācittiyapāli, Vipassana Reserach Institute, Dhammagiri, Igatputi, India: First Edition 1998; co-publisher, The Corporate Body of the Buddha Educational Foundation, Taipei.

Paṭṭhānapāli, Tr. Narada Thera, Buddhist Missionary Society, Kaula Lumpur, Malaysia: 1978 1st ed. 1963 also ed. & trans. Mahathera Narada (Calcutta: Mahabodhi Society of India, 1992).

Paramatthadīpanī, Vipassana Research Institute, Dhammagiri Igatpuri, India: First Edition 1998; co-publisher, The Corporate Body of the Buddha Educational Foundation, Taipei, Taiwan.

Paramatthajotika, ed. C.S. Upasaka, Nava Nalanda Mahavihara, Granthamala, 1978.

Saṃyuttanikāyo, Vipassana Research Institute, Dhammagiri, Igatpuri, India: First Edition 1998; co-publisher, The Corporate Body of the Buddha Educational Foundation, Taipei and also, ed. M.L. Feer, 5 vols. (London: PTS, 1884-91) First trans. C.A.F. Rhys Davids & S. Sumangala Thera; vol. 1; C.A.F. Rhys Davids & F.L. Woodward vol. II; F.L. Woodward vols. III, IV, V. *The Book of the Kindred Saying* (London: PTS, 1950-56).

Samantapāsādikā, Vipassana Research Institute, Dhammagiri Igatpuri, India: First Edition 1998; co-publisher, The Corporate Body of the Buddha Educational Foundation, Taipei, Taiwan and also ed. N. Tatiya, Nava Nalanda Mahavihara, 1965, and also Hevavitarana printing, Sinhala script, 1919, Mahabodhi Society of Sri Lanka. And also ed. N. Tatiya, Nava Nalanda Mahavihara, Granthamala, 1965.

Sumaṅgagavilāsinī, Vipassana Research Institute, Dhammagiri Igatpuri, India: First Edition 1998; co-publisher, The Corporate Body of the Buddha Educational Foundation, Taipei, Taiwan.

Suttanipātapāli, Vipassana Research Institute, Dhammagiri, Igatpuri, India: First Edition 1998; co-publisher, The Coporate Body of the Buddha Educational Foundation, Taipei, Taiwan and also, ed. V. Fausbell (London: PTS, 1885). Trans. K.R. Norman, *The Group of Discourses* (London: PTS, 1955-84).

The Long Discourses of Buddha, a Translation of the *Dīghanikāya* by Maurice Walshe; Buddhist Publication Society, Sangharaja Mawatha, Kandy, Sri Lanka 1996 (First Edition, Boston, Massachusetts USA: 1995).

Udānapāli, Vipassana Research Institute, Dhammagiri, Igatpuri, India: First Edition 1998; co-publisher, The Corporate Body of the Buddha Educational Foundation, Taipei, Taiwan.

Vibhaṅgapāli, Vipassana Research Institute, Dhammagiri Igatpuri, India: First Edition 1998; co-publisher, The Corporate Body of the Buddha Educational Foundation, Taipei, Taiwan.

Vimānavatthupāli, Vipassana Research Institute, Dhammagiri Igatpuri, India: First Edition 1998; co-publisher, The Corporate Body of the Buddha Educational Foundation, Taipei, Taiwan.

Visuddhimagga, Vipassana Research Institute, Dhammagiri Igatpuri, India: First Edition 1998; co-publisher, The Corporate Body of the Buddha Educational Foundation, Taipei, Taiwan and also, ed. Swami Dwaraka Dasa Sastri, Baudha Bharati, Baudha Bharati Series-12 (Varanasi, 1977). Tr. Bhikkhu Nanamoli, *The Path of Purification* Buddhist Publication Society (Kandy: 1991, 1st edn. 1956).

Canonical Texts Used in Sinhalese Script

Aṅguttara Nikāya, Buddha Jayanti Tipiṭaka Editorial Board, Government of Sri Lanka, Government Press, Colombo, 1961.

Cullavagga Pāli, Part I, Buddha Jayanti Tipiṭaka Editorial Board, Government of Sri Lanka, Government Press, Colombo, 1977.

Cullavagga Pāli, Part II, Buddha Jayanti Tipiṭaka Editorial Board, Government of Sri Lanka, Government Press, Colombo, 1977.

Dīgha Nikāya, Buddha Jayanti Tipiṭaka Editorial Board, Government of Sri Lanka, Government Press, Colombo, 1961.

Khuddaka Nikāya, Buddha Jayanti Tipiṭaka Editorial Board, Government of Sri Lanka, Government Press, Colombo, 1977.

Khuddakapāṭha Pāli, vol. I, Buddha Jayanti Tipiṭaka Editorial Board, Government of Sri Lanka, Government Press, Colombo, 1976.

Mahāvagga Pāli, Part I, Buddha Jayanti Tipiṭaka Editorial Board, Government of Sri Lanka, Government Press, Colombo, 1961.

Mahāvagga Pāli, Part II, Buddha Jayanti Tipiṭaka Editorial Board, Government of Sri Lanka, Government Press, Colombo, 1963.

*Majjhima Nikāya,*Buddha Jayanti Tipiṭaka Editorial Board, Government of Sri Lanka, Government Press, Colombo, 1964.

Milindapañha, Buddha Jayanti Tipiṭaka Editorial Board, Government of Sri Lanka, Government Press, Colombo, 1956.

Pācittiya Pāli, Part I, Buddha Jayanti Tipiṭaka Editorial Board, Government of Sri Lanka, Government Press, Colombo, 1981.

Pācittiya Pāli, Part II, Buddha Jayanti Tipiṭaka Editorial Board, Government of Sri Lanka, Government Press, Colombo, 1982.

*Paṭṭhānapāli,*Buddha Jayanti Tipiṭaka Editorial Board, Government of Sri Lanka, Government Press, Colombo, 1979.

Pārājika Pāli, vol. I, Buddha Jayanti Tipiṭaka Editorial Board, Government of Sri Lanka, Government Press, Colombo, 1980.

Parivāra Pāli, vol. I, Buddha Jayanti Tipiṭaka Editorial Board, Government of Sri Lanka, Government Press, Colombo, 1977.

Parivāra Pāli, vol. II, Buddha Jayanti Tipiṭaka Editorial Board, Government of Sri Lanka, Government Press, Colombo, 1977.

Saṃyutta Nikāya, Buddha Jayanti Tipiṭaka Editorial Board, Government of Sri Lanka, Government Press, Colombo, 1962.

Suttanipāta, Buddha Jayanti Tipiṭaka Editorial Board, Government of Sri Lanka, Government Press, Colombo, 1977.

SECONDARY SOURCES

Ācārya Tulsi, Trans: Satkari Mookerjee, *Illuminator of Jain Tenets,* (*Jain Siddānta Dīpikā*), Anekanta Sodha-Pitha Jain Vishva Bharari, Ladnun, Rajasthan (First Edition, 1985).

Adhikaram, E.W., *Early History of Buddhism in Ceylon,* Swabhasha Press, Colombo, 1946.

Ambedkar, B.R., *The Buddha and His Dhamma,* Siddahrath Publication, Bombay, 1974.

Banerjee, Satya Ranjan, *Prolegomena to Prakritica et Jainica,* The Asiatic Society, Kolakata, 2005.

Bapat, P.V., *2500 years of Buddhism,* First Published by on the occasion of 2500th anniversary of the Mahāparinibbāna of the Buddha, May 1956, Fifth Re-print September 1987, Published by Publication Division, Ministry of Information and Broadcasting Government of India.

Barua, Anomadarshi, *Itroduction to Pāli,* Bhartiya Vidya, Varanasi, Second revised and enlarged edition, 1977.

Barua, B.M., *Asoka and His Inscriptions,* New Age Publication, Calcutta, 1955.

Barua, R.B., *Theravāda Saṅgha,* The Asiatic Society of Bangladesh, 1974.

Basham, A.L., *The Wonder that was India,* Sidurick and Jakson, London, 1954.

Bhaskar, Bhagcandra Jain, *Jainism in Buddhist Literature,* Alok Prakashan, Nagpur India (First Edition: 1972).

Bhattacharya, B.C., *The History of Sāranāth,* Banaras, Rameshwar Patak, 1924.

Chatterjee and Duta, *An Introduction to Indian Philosophy,* 7th Edition, University of Calcutta 1968.

Combrich, R.F., *Precept and Practice,* Oxford, 1971.

Conzo, Edward, *Buddhist Thought in India,* London, George Allen and Unwin Ltd., 1962.

De Goukaldas, *Democracy in the Early Buddhist Saṅgha,* University Press, Calcutta, 1955.

Dutta, S., *Buddhist Monks and Monasteries of India,* George Allen, London, 1962.

Dutta, S., *Early Buddhist Monachism,* London, Kegan Paul Trench, 1924.

Ganesh Lalwani (ed.), Lalwani, K.C. (tr.), *Uvavaiya Suttaṁ,* Prakrit Bharati Academy, Jaipur First edition, 1988.

Geiger, Wilhelm, *Pāli Literature and Language,* Munshiram Manoharlal, New Delhi, 1978.

Hazra, Kanai Lal, *Pāli Language and Literature,* 2 vols., New Delhi, D.K. Printworld (P) Ltd.

Hirakava, Akira, *A Study of the Vinaya Piṭaka,* Tokyo, Sankibo Bussborin, 1960.

Horner, I.B., *Woman under Primitive Buddhism,* Motilal Banarsidass, Delhi.

Jain, Jyotiprasad, *Religion and Culture of the Jainas,* Bharatiya Jnanpith, Connaught Place, New Delhi, (First Edition, 1975).

Jain, R.C., *Samanya Jnana Digadarshana,* Upakara Prakashan, Agra, (enlarged edition, 2003).

Jain, R.C., *Upakāra Sāmānya Jñāna Digdarsan,* Upakāra Prakashan, Agra, 2003.

Jaina, Jagdish Chandra, *Prākrit Sāhitya Kā Itihāsa,* Published by Chaukhamba Vidya Bhavan, Delhi, Second Edition, 1985.

Jayatilaka, K.N., *The Message of the Buddha,* New York, The Free Press 1975.

Jha, L.K., *Man and the Moral Base,* New Bhararatiya Book Corporation, New Delhi, First edition, 2009.

Kalupahana, D.J., *Buddhist Philosophy,* A East West Centre Book, University Press, Hawaii.

Kem, H., *Manual of Indian Buddhism,* Indological Book House, Varanasi, 1972.

Khadabadi, B.K., *Śrāvakācāra,* (Jain code of conduct for Householder) Shri Raj Krisna Jain Charitable Trust, New Delhi, 1992.

Kogon Mizuno, *Beginning of Buddhism,* Kosei Publishing Co., Tokyo, 1980.

Kunthusagarjī, *Śrāvakadharmapradīpa,* Sanskrit and Hindi Commentator Pandita Jaganmohanlal Siddhartasastri, Published by Sri Ganesha Varni Digambara Jaina Sansthana, Naria, Varanasi, 2nd Edition, 1980.

Law, B.C., *A History of Pāli Literature,* London, Oxford University Press, 1933.

Malalasekara, G.P. *The Pāli Literature of Ceylon,* London, Royal Asiatic Society, 1928.

Mehta, Mohan Lal, *Outline of Jain Philosophy,* Jain Mission Society, Chikpet, Bangalore, 1954.

Mishra, Madhusudan, *Householder's Discipline in Jainism,* Eastern Book Linkers, Jawahar Nagar, Delhi, (First Edition, 1996).

Misra, G.P., *The Age of Vinaya,* New Delhi, Munishiram Manoharlal, 1972.

Morgan Kenneth, S.W., *The Path of Buddha*, New York, The Ronald Press, 1956.

Muni Nathamala, *Jaina Dharma and Darsana,* Setha Mannalalayi Surana Memorial Trust, Calcutta (First Edition), 1960.

Murti, T.R.V., *The Central Philosophy of Buddhism,* London, George Allen and Unwin, 1955.

Nagai, N., *Buddhist Vinaya Discipline or Commandments,* Calcutta Thacker, Spinck and Company, 1931.

Nagaraj Ji, Muni Shri, *Jain Philosophy and Modern Science,* Anuvrat Samiti, Kanpur (First Edition, 1959).

Nalinaksha Dutt, *Early Monastic Buddhism,* Firma KLM Private Ltd., Calcutta, 1981.

Obesekere Gananath, *The Two Wheels of Dhamma,* American and others Academy of Religious Studies, 1972.

Pachow, W., *The Prātimoksa-Sutta of the Mahāsaṅghikas,* Ganganatha Jha Research Institute, Allahabad.

Radhakrishnan, S., *The Hindu View of Life,* Indus An imprint of Harper Colins Publishers India Pvt. Ltd., New Delhi, Second impression 1994 (First Published 1927).

Rahula, W., *What the Buddha Thought,* Golden Fraser, Bedford, 1967.

Sarao, K.T.S., *Origin and Nature of Ancient Indian Buddhism,* Published by R&R Publishers, Delhi, First Edition 1989, Second Revised Edition, 1999.

Sharma, R.S., *Ancient India,* N.C.E.R.T., First Edition, August 1977,

Revised Edition, August 1980.

Sharma, R.S., *Ancient India,* published by N.C.E.R.T. (Reprint edition, First edition, 1977, Delhi, 1986)

Stcherbatsky, Th., *The Conception of Buddhist Nirvāna,* Leningrad Publishing Officer of the Academy of Science of the USSR, 1929.

Suddhatissa, H., *Buddhist Ethics, Essence of Buddhism,* London, George Allen and Unwin Ltd., 1970.

Tachipana, S., *The Ethics of Buddhism,* London Oxford University Press, 1926, reprinted, 1975.

Thomas, E.J., *The Road to Nirvāna: A Selection of the Buddhist Scriptures*, London, 1950.

Tiwary, Mahesh, *Perspective on Buddhist Ethics,* Published by Department of Buddhist Studies, University of Delhi, 1989.

Tomas, E.J., *The History of Buddhist Thought,* London, Kegan and Paul, 1935.

Tomas, J., *Early Buddhist Scripture,* London, Kegan and Paul, 1935.

Tomas, J., *Life of Buddha as Legend and History,* London 1949.

Upadhyaya, Bharata Singh, *Pali Sahitya ka Itihasa,* Hindi Sahitya Sammelan (Allahabad, 1986, 4th edn. 1st edn. 1951).

Vajirañāṇa, *Introduction to the Mahāvagga,* Buddha Jayanti Publication, Colombo.

Valisinha Devapriya, *Buddhist Shrines in India,* Colombo Mahabodhi Society, 1948.

Varma Vishwanath, P., *Early Buddhism and Its Origins,* New Delhi, Munshiram Manoharlal.

Varni, Jinendra, *Sama Suttam,* Bhagwan Mahavir Memorial Samiti, New Delhi, First Edition; 1993, Second Edition; 1999.

Verma, R.K. and Gopal Verma, *Research Methodology,* Published by Commonwealth Publishers, New Delhi, First Edition, 1989.

Verma, S. Bhagirati, *Socio-Religious, Economies and Literacy Condition of Bihar,* New Delhi, Munishiram Manoharlal.

Warder Anthony, K., *Indian Buddhism,* Delhi, Motilal Banarsidass, 1970.

Warren Henry Clarke, *Buddhism in Translations,* Cambridge, Harvard University Press, 1922.

Wickramasinghe, K.D.P., *The Biography of the Buddha,* Colombo, 1972.

Wijesekera, O.H. de A., *Knowledge and Conduct of Buddhist Philosophy and Ethics,* The Wheel Publication, Kandy.

Winternitz, Maurice, *History of Indian Literature,* Calcutta University Press, 1932.

Woodward, P.L., *Some Sayings of Buddha World's Classics*, Oxford, 1938.

Vesak Celebrations and Conference Programme

United Nations day of Vesak Conference 2008 in Vietnam 13-17 May 2008, National Convention Centre, Hanoi, Published International Organizing Committee, Vietnam, 2008. Cover page.

Dictionaries

Malalasekara, G.P., *Dictionary of Pāli Proper Names,* Motilal Banarsidass, (Pvt. Ltd.), first published in U.K. 1937, First Indian Edition, Delhi, 2007.

Monier-Williams, M., *Sanskrit-English Dictionary,* Motilal Banarsidass, Delhi, 1955, and Oxford University Press, 1889.

Rhys Davids, T.W. and William, *Pāli English Dictionary*, Motilal Banarsidass (Delhi, 1993 1st Indian Edition, 1st Published, London, 1921-25).

Upasaka, C.S., *Dictionary of Early Monastic Terms,* Varanasi, Bharati Prakashan, 1975.

Appendix 1

1. Sri Maha Bodhi Tree – Anuradhapura

2. Samadhi Statue - Polonnaruwa Gal-viharaya, Sri Lanka

3. Thuparama Pagoda, Anuradhapura, Sri Lanka

4. Kirivehera, Kataragama, Sri Lanka

5. A Buddhist Abet

6. The Sāmaṇera monk who are discussing the Dhamma

7. The Meditating Monks in Sri Lanka

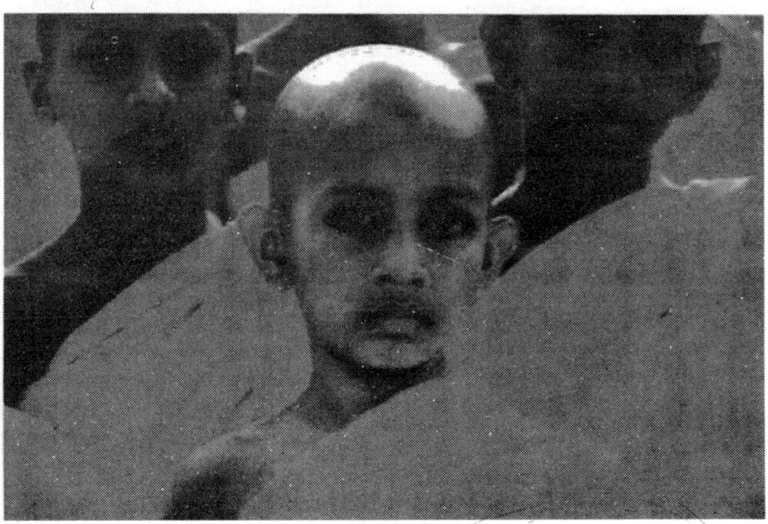

8. The little Sāmaṇera, Pepiliyana, Sri Lanka

9. An old lay devotee reading a Dhamma book

10. A Meditating Monk

11. Worshipping Buddhist Monk

12. Buddhist Monks and lay students in Education

Appendix 2

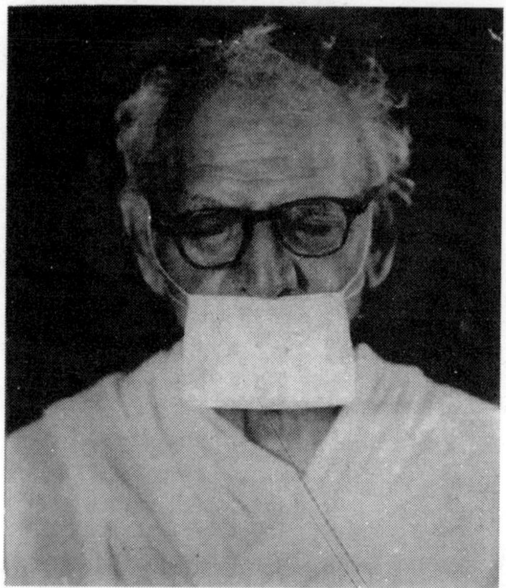

13. A Śvetāmbara Jain Monk from Punjab

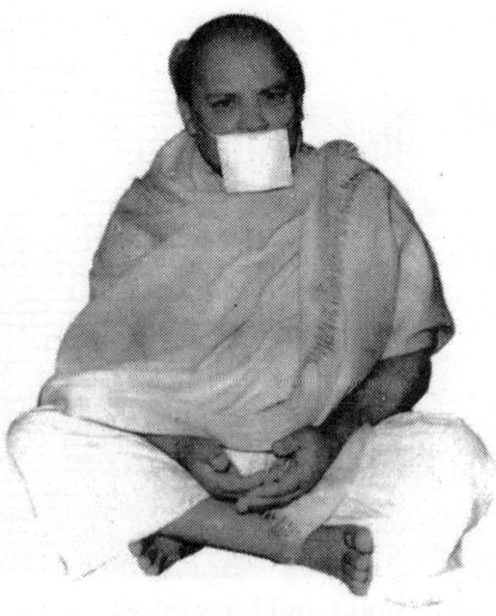

14. Shri Prem Sukh Ji Maharaj

15. A Śvetāmbara Jain Monk with his Broom

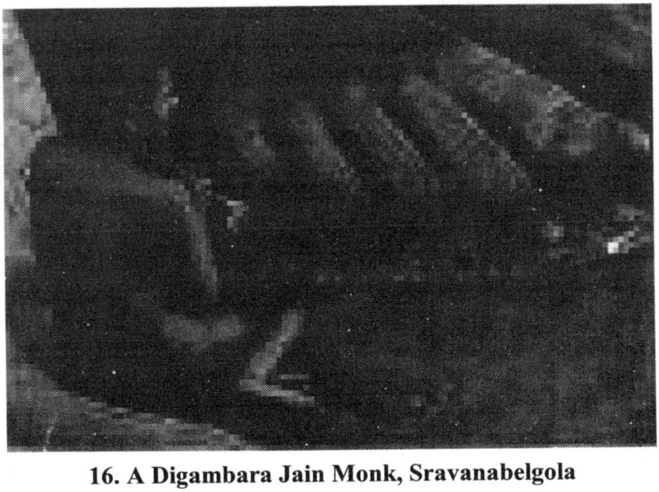

16. A Digambara Jain Monk, Sravanabelgola

17. Digambara Jain Monks in Sāranāth

18. A Jain Temple in Sāranāth

19. Jain Meditation, Chattarpur, India

Index